OCEAN LINER
POSTCARDS

OCEAN LINER
POSTCARDS
in Marine Art 1900-1945

ROBERT WALL

Antique Collectors' Club

©1998 Robert Wall
World copyright reserved

Reprinted 2000

ISBN 1 85149 275 5

British Library Cataloguing-in-Publication Data
A catalogue record for this book is available from the British Library

Printed in England
by the Antique Collectors' Club Ltd., Woodbridge, Suffolk
on Consort Royal Satin paper
supplied by the Donside Paper Company, Aberdeen, Scotland

Frontispiece: **Titanic** *(46,329 tons, White Star). The artwork of this card is
identical to No. 77 (see page 65), only the title being overprinted. The card
dates from December 1913, posted in Seymour, Wisconsin).*

Title page: **Sirius**, *the first steamship to carry fare-paying passengers from
Europe to North America in April 1838, just ahead of Brunel's Great Western.
(See page 18.)*

The Antique Collectors' Club

The **Antique Collectors' Club** was formed in 1966 and quickly grew to a five figure membership spread throughout the world. It publishes the only independently run monthly antiques magazine, *Antique Collecting*, which caters for those collectors who are interested in widening their knowledge of antiques, both by greater awareness of quality and by discussion of the factors which influence the price that is likely to be asked. The Antique Collectors' Club pioneered the provision of information on prices for collectors and the magazine still leads in the provision of detailed articles on a variety of subjects.

It was in response to the enormous demand for information on 'what to pay' that the price guide series was introduced in 1968 with the first edition of *The Price Guide to Antique Furniture* (completely revised 1978 and 1989), a book which broke new ground by illustrating the more common types of antique furniture, the sort that collectors could buy in shops and at auctions rather than the rare museum pieces which had previously been used (and still to a large extent are used) to make up the limited amount of illustrations in books published by commercial publishers. Many other price guides have followed, all copiously illustrated, and greatly appreciated by collectors for the valuable information they contain, quite apart from prices. The Price Guide Series heralded the publication of many standard works of reference on art and antiques. *The Dictionary of British Art* (now in six volumes), *The Pictorial Dictionary of British 19th Century Furniture Design, Oak Furniture* and *Early English Clocks* were followed by many deeply researched reference works such as *The Directory of Gold and Silversmiths,* providing new information. Many of these books are now accepted as the standard work of reference on their subject.

The Antique Collectors' Club has widened its list to include books on gardens and architecture. All the Club's publications are available through bookshops world wide and a full catalogue of all these titles is available free of charge from the addresses below.

Club membership, open to all collectors, costs little. Members receive free of charge *Antique Collecting*, the Club's magazine (published ten times a year), which contains well-illustrated articles dealing with the practical aspects of collecting not normally dealt with by magazines. Prices, features of value, investment potential, fakes and forgeries are all given prominence in the magazine.

Among other facilities available to members are private buying and selling facilities and the opportunity to meet other collectors at their local antique collectors' club. There are eight in Britain and more than a dozen overseas. Members may also buy the Club's publications at special pre-publication prices.

As its motto implies, the Club is an organisation designed to help collectors get the most out of their hobby: it is informal and friendly and gives enormous enjoyment to all concerned.

For Collectors — By Collectors — About Collecting

ANTIQUE COLLECTORS' CLUB
5 Church Street, Woodbridge Suffolk IP12 1DS, UK
Tel: 01394 385501 Fax: 01394 384434
Email: sales@antique-acc.com
Website: www.antique-com.com
or
Market Street Industrial Park, Wappingers' Falls, NY 12590, USA
Tel: 914 297 0003 Fax: 914 297 0068
E-mail: info@antiquecc.com
Website www.antiquecc.com

To my mother, Gladys Perina Wall,
who took me to see the *Queen Mary* in 1937,
and started my love of the ocean liner.

Contents

Introduction   9

CHAPTER 1   The Postcard in Marine History   10

CHAPTER 2   Notes for Collectors   14

CHAPTER 3   The Blue Riband Routes   17

CHAPTER 4   The Canadian Routes   88

CHAPTER 5   The South Atlantic   105

CHAPTER 6   India, The Indies, Australasia and the Far East 122

CHAPTER 7   The Postcard Artists   145

Bibliography   151

Abbreviations   151

Index   153

Introduction

Postal historians date the first use of postcards as 1 October 1869 and add that they were introduced into the United Kingdom in the following year. These were plain cards with the address written on one side and the message on the reverse. It was left to the Germans to print small illustrations on the corners of the message side, usually as some form of advertisement, and so was the picture postcard born.

Later in the century, the picture had grown to take over most of the message space but national post offices still insisted that only the address be carried on the reverse side. It was not until 1902 that the layout familiar today was allowed, i.e. the message and the address written on the reverse.

Picture postcards have always been collectable. Cheap and easy to come by, they soon build up in numbers. Earlier this century there were few British families that did not possess a postcard album. Often discarded in later years, these old albums can provide rich pickings for today's collector.

Shipping companies engaged in the passenger liner business started to use postcards in the mid-1890s. Not only were they an additional form of advertising but they were also an extra source of income. The simple phrase 'Send us a postcard', used as a farewell instruction to departing friends, kept many an artist from the breadline, contributed to the fiscal revenue and carried news, good or ill, to millions of recipients.

A good, colourful artist's impression, showing all the power and speed (often exaggerated!) of a big liner soon proved more attractive to the travelling public than the rather dull photographic cards of those days, so the postcard publishers and the liner companies sought out the services of artists who specialised in marine work to provide the subjects for their cards. Sometimes these were already established artists but more often they were poster illustrators working for printing companies engaged in the advertising business. Cards and postage stamps were available on board and on the dockside and there was scarcely an immigrant who did not send his or her loved one a farewell message. Hence on to the market flooded millions of cards and today their remnants provide a satisfying and reasonably inexpensive hobby for the marine postcard collector. Because the liner companies often engaged the top marine artists of the day (Dixon and Spurling are good examples), some of the cards are masterpieces in their own right and eminently collectable.

As it happened, the author started his own collection quite inadvertently in the early 1940s when he was given about forty White Star Line cards by the then art master at Monmouth School, the late Marcus Holmes. Holmes was a considerable watercolourist in his own right and he used the cards as examples as he attempted to drum something of form and line into a group of schoolboys whose minds were out on the rugger pitch or far away with older brothers on active service. At the end of his last term at Monmouth, when he retired, Holmes handed the collection on to a young liner enthusiast who has remained grateful for his generosity and has cherished his memory down the years.

This book attempts to introduce the collecting of ocean liner postcards to the general reader and also to the enthusiast. It uses artists' cards to illustrate a general history of the major liner companies and adds a commentary on the artists and their work, a short note on publishers and a guide to collectors who may care to take up this fascinating hobby.

Robert Wall
Port of Bristol, 1998

CHAPTER 1

The Postcard in Marine History

The use of the postcard as a method of communication dates from the 1870s although the first picture postcard appeared in Great Britain less than one hundred years ago.

On 1 October 1870 the General Post Office began to issue a plain postcard with a stamp already printed on it. The rules for the use of this postcard were rigidly enforced and the postage rates were ½d for the United Kingdom including Ireland and 1¼d for overseas. The address had to be written on the stamped side while the message was carried on the plain reverse.

This situation continued until 1 September 1894 when the Post Office finally allowed private postcards to be dispatched through their postal system using an adhesive ½d stamp. During this time a fashion had developed in Europe for picture postcards, mainly carrying patriotic motifs and messages. It is alleged that the Franco-Prussian war of 1870 had much to do with the start of postcard sending and that this led in the 1880s and '90s to holiday makers, particularly in Switzerland, sending greeting cards to the families remaining at home. All these cards had the picture and message on the one side with the address and stamp on the other and are known today to the collector as 'undivided backs'.

The British Post Office first allowed the dispatch of picture postcards on 1 October 1894. Until then only trade messages or printed detail from companies had been allowed on the 'message' side and, while the results are very interesting to the deltiologist – the collector of postcards – they have little attraction. In this year of 1894 a Scottish company, George Stewart and Co. of Edinburgh, published the first British postcards with views and many other firms soon followed their example. However, the postal regulations still required that the message was written on the same side as the picture and the current standard size of postcard, known as a court card, gave only a space of 4¾ x 3¾ inches to carry the picture and also the message.

Companies persevered with this size until 1899 when the standard postcard size in use today, 5½ x 3½ inches, was introduced. The restrictions on the address side, however, were retained and it was not until January 1902, when the GPO reached agreement with European Post Offices, that the 'divided back' card was accepted for postal use. This reform allowed the whole of the front of the postcard to be used for the picture and for the back to be divided in half, partly for the message and the remainder for the address. General use started in October 1902.

From that day in 1902, the postcard rapidly developed into a very popular form of communication. Postcards were cheap to buy and postage equally inexpensive. People were attracted to the little cards in an age which had yet to see mass colour photography, the cinematograph or television. The Post Office also gave a service which in London amounted to six deliveries a day. It was, therefore, possible to post a card at nine o'clock in the morning and know that your correspondent would receive it at midday. The files of postcard dealers are full of examples of this type of use and it is a fascinating speculation to examine messages on cards and to note the many varied times of posting that the postmarks indicate. Anything from 6.30 a.m. to midnight can be found on British postcards, the cancellation stamp defacing the benign features of King Edward VII in the attractive green ½d stamp used in those days.

This heyday of the postcard lasted from 1902 until the outbreak of the First World War in 1914. Every kind of subject was published and transport was particularly popular. Early aircraft postcards were very much in demand. Locomotives and railways, paddle steamers and piers and all kinds of shipping subjects soon flooded on to the market. As the cards piled up in the homes of people, so collections were started and there were very few families in the first decade of this century who did not possess a picture postcard album. Good examples of these fetch high prices at auction. So vast was the postcard traffic that in the fiscal year 1908-9 eight hundred and sixty million cards were handled by the GPO in Britain alone.

To the shipowner, the introduction of the picture postcard was a godsend. By the 1890s, the most lucrative routes for the passenger liner operator were on the North Atlantic. The American industrial expansion was at its height and the emerging industries of Pittsburgh, Detroit and Chicago were seeking labour from any source from which it could be obtained. In addition, the nation was expanding into the mid-west at a startling rate. This meant that large ships from Europe, carrying anything up to one thousand immigrants at a time, were cheap to operate and very profitable. On the eastbound run the same liners carried hundreds of prosperous Americans, newly rich and eager to seek their roots in Europe or go on what was known as the 'Grand Tour' of cities in the old continent.

Apart from the postcard, the only advertising media available to the shipping companies were the newspapers and such poster work that could be done around ports and agents' offices. Hence the postcard became an important method of circulating news of services and publicising particular liners. Almost every immigrant who could write sent his farewell messages on postcards to families remaining behind and these, as they passed from hand to hand, were useful vehicles for carrying the shipping company's message to its customers.

Consequently, postcard publishers worked closely with shipping companies to produce whole series of cards. Publishers like A. Reid of Newcastle upon Tyne, who specialised in P&O ships, and F.G.O. Stuart of Southampton, who published for Union Castle Line, soon emerged as leading the business. The giant publisher of liners at this time was, however, Tuck whose 'Celebrated Liners Series' is still sought after by collectors today. American Line and Cunard were prominent in the series entitled 'Hands Across the Sea' which exploited the nostalgia

that most families felt for friends settled in the dominions and colonies.

Anyone examining the correspondence of these immigrants, as shown in their short messages written on the postcards they dispatched, will soon find references to the size of the 'boat' on which they were about to sail. Size and speed were two valuable commodities on which the market position of any particular liner was based. Of its very nature, size spelt safety and speed meant that the voyager probably spent less time on the ocean, and therefore less time suffering from seasickness which was the great fear of any Edwardian sea passenger. This latter subject is also referred to in much postcard correspondence.

In order to get the impression of size, dignity and speed, the postcard publishers turned away from real photographs, which often appeared grey and dull, showing the ship in the distance. It was difficult to take the large and unwieldy cameras of those days into a boat and so position yourself to obtain a good photograph of a liner at sea and at speed. Therefore, the publishers turned to marine artists to create impressions for them and thus was the colour ship postcard born.

Initially, the publishers went to the leading marine artists of the day. These were usually found working in the principal ports, where their skills were used by shipowners for posters and advertising work. Quite frequently the artist could pick up commissions from officers and members of crew for oil paintings of the ship in which they were currently serving. Higher standard pictures were demanded for the boardrooms of the big shipping companies and, fortunately, some of these have been preserved to this day.

Although Charles Dixon was London based, many of the postcard artists lived and worked in Liverpool. Prominent among these were Sam J.M. Brown, J.S. Mann, Odin Rosenvinge, Kenneth Shoesmith and Walter Thomas. All these artists were born between 1880 and 1894. Rosenvinge particularly made Cunard Liners his speciality and did much work for that company, while Dixon and Thomas, supported by Montague Black, produced excellent work for the White Star Line which operated out of

Liverpool for much of its transatlantic work until 1907 when it moved its big liners to Southampton.

The demand for cabin space on the Atlantic was supplemented by the empire routes, both from the British Isles and from Europe, to the colonies that the major powers were establishing in Africa, Asia and Australasia. Advertising became critical to the success of the business and, together with new lithographic techniques, led to the foundation of the big advertising agencies that we know today. Many of the marine artists working for shipping companies were engaged on producing the colourful posters that appeared on billboards nationwide, extolling the comfort and excellence of the promoters' fleet. Competition was fierce and because the advertising was aimed at people who were not generally expected to be found in the first class of an ocean liner these techniques became in themselves instruments for social change. A whole generation of European workers, frustrated by unemployment and old social attitudes, simply transferred their loyalties to the United States and in doing so made fortunes for the shipowners while at the same time changing the shape of social structures and attitudes in a dramatic fashion.

It was no difficulty for the poster artist to turn his attention to postcards. In fact, a postcard was quick to produce and any artist with a confident technique could produce a good impression of an ocean liner. Commissions were eagerly sought and such artists as Dixon were always in demand. It is an interesting speculation today to wonder at the fate of the original artwork for many of these posters. The P&O Company still possesses some of the splendid originals by Jack Spurling and Dixon's work comes frequently on the market, where £6,000 is not considered expensive these days for an original. Most of the other artists seldom appear in the salerooms and the original work must have been long destroyed. Anything by Sam Brown or Odin Rosenvinge that does reach the saleroom inevitably commands high prices.

All through the Edwardian decade, postcards of liners flooded on to the market. Then, as the decade ended, shipowners began to discover a new use for some of their vessels. Taking a coastal voyage as a holiday in its own right was already quite popular in areas where the seaboard had scenic attractions like the islands and lochs of Scotland and the Dalmatian coast of the Adriatic. In Scotland, the principal company was David MacBrayne who pioneered holidays using ships for touring, giving rise to the Scottish adage 'The earth is the Lord's and all that therein is – except the Western Highlands which belong to MacBraynes'.

Another favourite holiday route was up the Norwegian coast from Bergen to the North Cape but in the early days this journey entailed going ashore to spend the night. The large ocean liners offered spaciousness and luxury with plentiful accommodation and so was the cruise liner born. The first destination were the fiords of Norway and the classical sights of the Mediterranean. So another market for the postcard was created.

The enthusiasm for postcards of any subject continued into the early 1920s, although the restrictions on paper supplies during the First World War led to shortages of cards and this was followed by steep increases in postal charges both in 1918 and 1919. By the latter year, the postage on postcards had trebled but enthusiasm continued.

The United States Government decided in 1924 to commence immigration control. This had a dramatic effect on the number of passengers sailing from Europe to the United States and this, in its turn, started the decline of the marine postcard. This fact, coupled with the installation of the private telephone in ever increasing numbers and the flexibility of travel which could be obtained from the motor car, led to a steep decline in the use of postcards by the shipping companies although some of the best work produced came out at the end of the '20s and throughout the '30s. The latter decade is important for the emergence of Charles Turner who worked for Cunard producing some of the highest quality postcards published by a shipping company.

The Second World War ended the heyday of the marine artist postcard. The arrival of total war and the complete control of raw materials led to a virtual cessation of production, although cards of warships, aeroplanes and other military themes were allowed for propaganda purposes. When war ended, the colour photograph had so improved in quality that this medium was to become the most popular way of producing postcards for shipping. Nevertheless, one or two artists still sold their work to shipping companies and the work of Derrick Smoothy and John Nicholson continues to be used to this day. Other post-war artists include Turner who did a superb series for Cunard in the late '40s and early '50s. Continental companies also commissioned artists and there are a number of cards available produced in the late '60s from French and Italian companies such as Messageries Maritime and the Italia Line.

Elsewhere the colour photograph, produced from transparencies and printed to a very high standard, had taken over from the artist's impression. The availability of the light-weight miniature camera, used afloat in high speed launches and fitted with high performance lenses, allowed the photographer to obtain pictures of the big ships which showed off all their colourful grace and size in the same manner and style as the old-time ship illustrator. Foremost in the field of this new type of postcard was the Isle of Wight based publisher J. Arthur Dixon, who produced a series of colour postcards in the '60s which remain among the best ocean liner postcards ever published.

These years of the late '60s and early '70s saw the withdrawal from service of the last liners used on the traditional ocean passenger routes. The international commuter has long transferred his patronage to the convenient time-saving and cheap fares offered by the airlines and the Cunard *Queens*, the *France*, the *United States* and the two Italian giants *Michelangelo* and *Rafaello* were all laid up at this time. To many shipping commentators it appeared that the day of the large ocean liner had passed but, as the '80s approached, the big ship achieved an astonishing metamorphosis.

Shipping practice in the '50s and '60s had suggested that the most suitable ship for cruising was somewhere between 20,000 and 30,000 gross tons, capable of fifteen knots average and carrying about five hundred passengers. Indeed, when Cunard attempted to use the *Queen Elizabeth* for cruising, her 80,000 ton bulk blundered around the Caribbean but attracted few passengers and huge financial losses. It was left to the American cruise market, developing largely in the Florida port of Miami, to produce the giant cruise liner, purpose-built to carry up to 2,000 passengers in absolute luxury. The Norwegians pioneered the American cruise market, using small ships operating out of Miami which was connected by air to all major centres in the United States and stood at the gateway to the Caribbean.

Between 1975 and 1980 the demand for cruise space doubled and the Norwegians were joined in the market by other European lines, usually employing second-hand tonnage registered in Liberia or Panama. In 1979, the Kloster concern of Oslo, trading as Norwegian Caribbean Lines, bought the French C.G.T. liner *France* which had been laid up in Le Havre and, after a rapid refit in Bremerhaven, sent her cruising with the new name *Norway*, sailing out of Miami. After initial problems, particularly with water systems, the big 60,000-tonner settled down to a successful second career and remains in commission today. She has been followed into service by a number of very large ships, of which P&O's *Royal Princess* is a good example. Royal Caribbean's *Sovereign of the Seas* is even larger than the *Norway* and the largest passenger ship in commission when introduced. A series of giants followed in the early '90s until, in 1996, Cunard's *QE2* was the twenty-sixth largest passenger ship.

Today's cruise passenger still remains loyal to old custom and dispatches postcards in vast quantity. International postage rates are no longer cheap and high quality colour printing costs have increased considerably. Nevertheless, the postcard is still an attractive method of telling friends back home that all is well and that one is having one helluva good time!

So, with millions of postcards, old and new, waiting to be collected, the opportunities for the ocean liner collector are immense. The next chapter will set out a few hints on how to collect.

CHAPTER 2

Notes for Collectors

The collection and study of postcards is defined as an exact science, 'cartology' (in the USA 'deltiology' and in France 'cartophilisme'), but when a collector is asked his opinion on the type of card which proves most valuable or most popular, then there is seldom any agreement. The amount of material waiting to be collected amounts to many millions of cards world-wide, and there are thousands of examples of shipping postcards awaiting the attention of the enthusiast. It is, therefore, useful to lay down a few basic rules on the subject to guide ourselves and others so that we are able to achieve our objectives, i.e. a good quality collection of shipping postcards illustrated by artists. This is as opposed to collecting real photographs of ships, which can also prove to be a satisfying and never-ending pursuit.

Many collectors of shipping postcards run several collections in parallel. It is possible to build up a collection of real postcards and you may wish to break these down into specialist themes, for example warships and merchant ships. Both these subjects classify into the various types of vessel that make up the general theme and some collectors specialise in just one area, for example trawlers, tugs or destroyers. It is probably better to collect a good quality collection on one particular theme than to amass a large amount of uncollated material. However, because the hobby is flexible, that is up to your own personal decision.

Your next rule is to get yourself some general knowledge about the subject. The bibliography lists postcard books which I have found interesting, and most public libraries carry a selection of recent postcard books in their arts section. Make a study of these and you will be surprised by the wide variety of advice on publishers and prices which appear in the various books in print today.

Nevertheless, reading two or three of them will be helpful and the current edition of one of the postcard catalogues available on the market will also help, although the shipping section is usually limited.

HOW TO COLLECT

There are three ways that the postcard collector can accumulate a collection. The first of these is to attend a postcard fair, the second is to be supplied direct from a dealer and the third is to attend a postcard auction. In these days of high inflation and rapidly rising prices, it is important that you spend your money wisely and that care is exercised, and, most importantly, time is taken to study properly the cards you have in mind to purchase.

Postcard fairs are held all around the country and are usually advertised in local newspapers. Most promoters of fairs run a mailing list and many who attend the fair ask at the door to be added to the mailing list if such exists. Fairs vary in size downwards from the very big international events such as the British International Postcard Exhibition which is held annually in London in September and the International Postcard Dourfe held in New York each May. Allow yourself plenty of time at fairs as each dealer will have a shipping section and will allow you to go through it card by card.

As you gain experience you will notice that the price of cards can vary considerably and the card offered by one dealer for £5 may well be found next week at a different fair for less than half that price. You have to develop experience of dealers. Some dealers carry only first class stock and charge accordingly. Others have thousands of cards where the quality will vary considerably. When you have thoroughly examined the card for quality only then should you buy it if you think the price is right.

Many cards come postally unused and are

therefore clean on the reverse. However, those that have been postally used can provide fascinating information about the sender or the addressee and the date stamp will give you a clear indication of where the ship was at that time. This is, of course, unless 'the pacquebot' cancellation stamp has been used, together with the national postage stamp of the ship's country of origin.

Many dealers will offer cards on approval and addresses of specialist dealers can be obtained from a good postcard catalogue. For shipping enthusiasts this is one of the catalogues' great values. Catalogues will also give you the dates of fairs and their locations.

Postcard auctions are held regularly in most centres in the U.K. and are run by local and national auction houses. While most of these auction companies specialise in a wide range of antiques, some of them do hold specialist postcard auctions and these are worth attending.

Again, give yourself time to inspect the goods on offer thoroughly beforehand. Then decide on the price you can afford to pay and do not get carried away at the auction by paying way over the odds at a figure you may regret later. Set a figure for each lot you intend to buy and don't exceed that. Never trust the auctioneer's description of the quality of a lot but inspect it personally at preview. Never buy blind. Never rely on any price estimate even though you know the auctioneer has some expertise on postcard prices. Sometimes the valuation given in the catalogue is given to hype the price. Never buy a vast collection of cards of variable quality simply by averaging the quantity of the collection against the price. Go for clearly identified lots of the type of card that you require for your collection.

WHAT TO LOOK FOR!

The number of shipping cards available in Great Britain is immense but collectors seem to go down very well chosen tracks in searching out the rarities which appeal to them. If you eliminate the many thousands of photographic cards the number of cards to look for is greatly reduced and artists' cards are comparatively rare compared with photographs.

The cards produced by Andrew Reid and Co.

of Newcastle upon Tyne in the first decade of this century are always expensive. Personally, I do not find them highly attractive, but they are interesting museum pieces in terms of the chromo-lithograph process and, if used postally, can contain interesting messages and attractive date stamps. The second most sought after cards are those issued by companies for advertising and these can also attract high prices. Then follow the general colour artist postcards which the collector must decide for himself on which to specialise. It is a good idea to collect by company and collectors deciding to collect the Cunard and White Star, or both, can build up a nice collection if they can afford it. As a guide to prices, the following average prices were paid during the summer of 1997:

I	Andrew Reid, Newcastle	£8 - £15
II	advertising cards	£10 - £15
III	artists' cards such as Turner	
	pictures on Forman cards	£5 - £10
IV	later cards i.e.	
	post-World War Two	£1 - £2

The above figures are a very general guide and all collectors are advised to hunt around. Original "Titanic" cards go for £75 plus.

PUBLISHERS

Of many hundreds of postcard publishers, the following is a list of those identified as major firms engaged in shipping publishing:

J. Birch – Southampton
J. Arthur Dixon – I.O.W.
Thomas Forman – Nottingham
Gale & Polden – Aldershot
F. Hartmann – London
C.R. Hoffmann – Southampton
Millar & Long – Glasgow
Andrew Reid & Co. –
    Newcastle upon Tyne
J. Salmon & Co. – Sevenoaks
F.G.O. Stuart – Southampton
Taylor, Garnett & Evans – Liverpool
Raphael Tuck – London & New York
    OILETTE 'Celebrated Liners Series'
    Serial Nos.

American Line	9140
Allan Line	9213

Atlantic Transport	9126
Canadian Pacific	9121, 9682
Cunard	9106, 9268
Dominion Line	9155
Hamburg-Amerika	9125
NDL Bremen	9124
Orient Pacific	6229
Royal Mail	9151
Union Castle	9133
White Star Line	6228, 9215, 9898

Turner & Dunnett – Liverpool
James Valentine & Sons, Dundee

NOTE: The above list is not exhaustive. It should also be remembered that many shipping companies (for example, P&O, Royal Mail, Union Castle and White Star) acted as their own publishing company. P&O cards of later years (Period 3 – see below) carry the company's coat of arms on the reverse side, as do Royal Mail's.

NUMBER OF CARDS ISSUED

In his book *Collecting Picture Postcards – an Introduction,* Anthony Byatt argues that, of cards published world-wide between 1895 and 1915, only 1% survive today. But as the total published was 140,000 million cards, approximately 1,400 million cards remain for today's collectors. Sales plunged after World War One and hence production fell off. Collectors categorise issue periods thus:

1870 - 1900	Period 1
1900 - 1920	Period 2
1920 - 1939	Period 3
1940 - 1970	Period 4
1970 - onwards	Period 5

CHAPTER 3

The Blue Riband Routes

The history of ocean liners begins with Brunel, the great British innovator and engineer. To claim that Brunel invented the steam engine, screw propeller and the use of metal for ship construction would be untrue, but he did take all three techniques and use them in the design of a prototype ocean liner which first took to the water in 1843 as the *Great Britain.* The idea of mechanical propulsion for ships is almost as old as man himself. The paddle, and later the oar, were in use before sail and the Egyptians, Greeks and Romans all used mass manpower on banks of oars to take their wooden warships into battle.

Isambard Kingdom Brunel was born at Portsmouth, England, in 1806 and showed an early skill in mathematics. At seventeen he entered his father's office as an assistant engineer and worked on the first Thames tunnel. He emerged as an engineer of importance in 1831 when his design for a bridge across the River Avon at Bristol was accepted. In 1833 he was appointed Engineer to the Great Western Railway and at a board meeting in October 1835 it is alleged that he urged the company that the railway line 'be continued to New York' by transferring the passengers to an ocean steamship at Bristol. Thus was the idea of the Great Western Steam Ship Company formed.

The ship herself emerged as the famous *Great Western* of 1837 and it was this ship that can really be called the first liner, in that she maintained a regular service between Bristol and New York during the years 1838 to 1842 and then from Liverpool until 1847. The ship was built in Bristol and engined on the Thames. She sailed on her maiden voyage on Sunday 8 April 1838 and crossed to New York in fifteen days ten and a half hours, only five hours behind her rival, the *Sirius* (No. 1) which had set out five days ahead.

The owners of the *Great Western* were an offshoot of the Great Western Railway Company and this may have some bearing on what happened next. The *Great Western* needed consorts to maintain a regular service and, more importantly, to land the lucrative mail contract to North America which was offered for tender in this same year of 1838.

Encouraged by Brunel, the Great Western Company laid down the largest ship in the world at Bristol, made of iron and screw propelled. Meanwhile, a Canadian from Halifax called Sam Cunard tendered for the mail contract with four ships roughly similar in size and speed to the *Great Western.*

The new Bristol ship, the famous *Great Britain* of 1843, absorbed all the resources that the Great Western Company could spare. Problems abounded and it was no surprise when Cunard's offer appeared more acceptable to the British Government and he got the lucrative mail contract.

To meet the terms of the contract, Cunard produced his first ocean liner, the famous *Britannia,* built at Port Glasgow by Robert Duncan and Company and with Napier engines. The Cunard Line's service to North America was inaugurated on 4 July 1840, the 64th Anniversary of the Declaration of Independence, and the Company that Cunard founded remains active in the steamship market to this day.

Cunard prospered and made money. Winter and summer, his red-funnelled ships ran in all weathers with splendid reliability. Technical advances allowed him to build his last wooden ship, the *Arabia* of 1852, and then the splendid sisters *Persia* in 1856 and *Scotia* in 1862 which, while being the first iron ships in the fleet, were also the last to be driven by paddle-wheels.

1. **Sirius** *(703 tons, British and American Steam Navigation Co.) was the first steamship to carry fare-paying passengers from Europe to North America in April 1838, just ahead of Brunel's* Great Western. *(Artist: Norman Wilkinson. Publisher: White Star)*

Throughout the '70s and '80s Cunard built a steady business until in 1884 they produced two record holders called *Umbria* and *Etruria* which outclassed all their rivals on the North Atlantic in size and capacity (Nos. 21 and 22). Within four years these ships had been challenged by the Inman Line's beautiful *City of New York* and *City of Paris* and also by the White Star Line's *Teutonic* and *Majestic* (No. 71).

Things never rested for long on the North Atlantic in those days and by 1893 Cunard had produced their largest ships to date, the *Campania* (Nos. 23 and 24), and her sister ship *Lucania*. Both these ships were record breakers from the start and they ruled the North Atlantic until 1897 when the North German Lloyd introduced their first four-funnelled liner and took the record away from Cunard. Cunard did not reply immediately as the Company was relatively satisfied with its four big liners on the New York service. Instead it developed secondary services running between Boston and New York to Mediterranean ports. The main objective of this service was to take

Americans on vacation to Europe and return loaded with emigrants, a trade that was beginning to develop into a very profitable business.

As the nineteenth century faded, the infant American republic had come of age and taken her place as one of the world's most powerful and economically prosperous nations. The long march westward was over, the bloody agony of civil war forty years behind and the railways now carried the wealth of the industrial north to the four corners of the American continent. The unprecedented economic expansion in the United States between 1865 and 1900 caused an immediate shortage of the one prime commodity that America did not possess – people. At the same time such European social disasters as the famine in Ireland, rebellion and civil strife in the Balkans and Eastern Europe, allied to abject poverty in the Latin countries, particularly Italy, caused a stream of emigrants to turn their eyes westward and sail for the New World.

The huge emigrant trade brought prosperity

2. **Britannic** *(5,004 tons, White Star) and* Germanic *were both Blue Riband holders from 1876 onwards. This card is a modern reproduction of a poster used to advertise sailings.*
(Trans-Atlantic Publishing Company)

to the shipping lines on the North Atlantic, while in the opposite direction a demand rose from prosperous Americans for luxury travel to Europe. On the North Atlantic, therefore, a multi-million dollar passenger trade grew up and the big shipping companies which engaged in this traffic prospered and grew.

Much American money was invested in the new shipping lines. A typical example was the White Star Line (to which we shall refer later) which, although British registered and manned, was wholly owned by the American tycoon J. Pierpoint Morgan. By 1900 Morgan had control of most of the big American and British companies on the Atlantic with the exception of Cunard.

Morgan's intervention in the shipping market coincided with the ultimate develop-ment of the reciprocating steam engine. As ships grew in size the demand for more power caused the designer to increase greatly the size of his engines. These massive forgings affected the whole ship. The largest set of reciprocating engines ever built went into the German liner

Kronprinzessin Cecilie in 1904, but it was obvious that the reciprocating engine had reached the end of its possible development.

A new source of power was required and it came from the ideas of Charles Parsons, a British engineer who invented a steam turbine in 1884. Parsons put his new turbine into a little yacht which passed among the assembled warships in the 1897 Spithead review of the British fleet. Their Lordships sent their latest torpedo boat destroyer to chase Parsons' boat away but she left the Naval vessel standing. The point had been made and immediate experiments on other ships were carried out.

The first transatlantic liner to use turbines, the Allan Line's vessel *Virginian* (see Nos. 121 and 123), came out in 1904. Cunard was already building two large intermediate liners, the *Caronia* (No. 25) and the *Carmania* (Nos. 15, 26 to 28 and 56). *Carmania* was hastily re-engined with turbine machinery and the key decision was taken to engine two new big liners with turbine machinery also. Contracts for these two vessels were placed respectively on

3. **City of Chester** *(4,556 tons, Inman) was built in 1873 in Greenock for the Liverpool owner, William Inman. She was the line's first two-funnelled ship, seen here in a contemporary advertising poster.*
(Trans-Atlantic Publishing Company)

the Tyne and the Clyde, with orders going to Swan Hunter and the Clydebank yard of John Brown and Company. The two ships were to become the immortal *Mauretania* (Nos. 30-31 and 57) and her sister *Lusitania* (No. 29).

The *Titanic* apart, the *Mauretania* of 1907 is arguably the most famous ship ever built. At 31,938 tons she was far and away the largest ship in the world at the time and dwarfed her German rivals. She clipped almost a whole day off the Atlantic speed record, her best passage before the First World War was four days, ten hours and fifty-one minutes at an average speed of 26.06 knots, a record she held for twenty-two years and which remains a most brilliant achievement in modern naval architecture.

The *Mauretania* and *Lusitania* were built with a large subsidy from the British Government which was very concerned about the American control of many of the British shipping lines. Such was the nature of European politics in those days that great suspicion was held of the German empire and its ambitious Kaiser, William II. The

Government concluded that large liners which could operate as either troop ships or auxiliary cruisers in wartime were a good investment for defence policy and loaned Cunard £2,600,000 at 2¾% repayable over a period of twenty years. This agreement was concluded in 1903 and also arranged for a twenty year subsidy of £150,000 per annum to be paid to Cunard because of the high standard of construction that the British Admiralty required in the new ships. Both parties to the bargain must have been well satisfied with the arrangements.

Following the two big four-funnel liners, Cunard added two smaller ships to their fleet in 1911, of which one was *Franconia* (No. 35), and then, just before the outbreak of the First World War they commissioned the *Aquitania* (Nos. 36 to 38 and 58), a beautiful four-funnel liner which was laid down as a reply to three big German vessels currently under construction. The maiden voyage of the *Aquitania* took place just before the outbreak of war in May 1914.

The four years of the First World War cost

4. *Norddeutscher Lloyd official postcard issued at the end of the century. The ship is possibly* **Stuttgart** *(5,048 tons) built in Fairfield, Glasgow in 1889.* (NDL)

Cunard in all twenty-two ships. By far and away the most famous and the most tragic of these losses was when U-22 torpedoed and sank *Lusitania* off the Old Head of Kinsale on 15 May, 1915.

The *Lusitania* incident remains controversial to this day. At the time the Germans alleged that she was carrying explosives from the United States to aid the British War effort but these claims were largely dismissed as propaganda by people in Great Britain and the United States. Today most writers are persuaded that, although U-20 fired only a single torpedo a second explosion occurred almost immediately. This could be explained by a boiler room explosion but some critics are prepared to concede that it may have been coal-dust exploding. However, in twenty minutes it was all over. *Lusitania* went down with the loss of 1,198 lives which included 124 United States citizens. Immediately, international controversy flared. Britain accused Germany of violation of international law and a wave of public indignation swept Britain and America

which did much to prepare American public opinion for a declaration of war by President Wilson in 1917.

Following the armistice in November 1918, Cunard required replacement tonnage urgently. This the company found in acquiring the giant German liner *Imperator* and at the same time placed orders for thirteen new ships as soon as was possible. At the time, this was the largest tonnage order ever placed by a single company.

The *Imperator* was renamed *Berengaria* (Nos. 39 to 41 and 59) and she became the Cunard flagship until the arrival of the *Queen Mary* in the 1930s. Throughout the 1920s until 1925 a whole series of Cunard intermediate liners joined the fleet. The first of these was *Albania* (No. 42) and she was closely followed by *Samaria* (Nos. 43 and 61), *Scythia* (Nos. 44, 45 and 60) and *Laconia* (Nos. 46, 47 and 62). At this time also, all Cunard liners were converted to oil fuel and the dreadful conditions of the stokeholds in coal-burning liners became a thing of the past. Cunard's replacement programme continued in 1923 with *Franconia*

5. **Karlsruhe** *(5,057 tons, NDL), another early official card from Norddeutscher Lloyd. The ship dates from 1889 and was scrapped in 1908.* *(NDL)*

(Nos. 53 and 55), *Lancastria* (No. 52) and the A-class liners of which *Andania* was the first to enter service stock (Nos. 18 and 48 to 51).

The strength and power of the Cunard fleet of the 1920s was graphically illustrated in a beautiful series of postcards prepared by the artist Charles Turner for the publishers Taylor, Garnett and Evans of Liverpool which Cunard issued in the late 1920s. These cards were all in the vertical configuration and are illustrated in Nos. 56 to 63.

Later in the same decade of the '20s, the Cunard line began to plan replacements for its ageing 'Big Three' liners. In 1930 it laid down on the Clyde an 80,000 ton giant to be built by John Brown and Company as their No. 534. The ship was no sooner started than the Company was hit by the economic depression of those years. Falling passenger figures on the Atlantic and a loss of trade caused work on the new liner to be held up. The future looked grim until the British Government intervened and, in exchange for a subsidy to continue the construction of the new ship, ordered a merger of Cunard and White Star, its principal British

competitor. The main result of this deal was the commissioning of the *Queen Mary* (No. 65), an 80,000 ton superliner whose name went into the English language and which is remembered with affection today. The words *Queen Mary* became a synonym for anything that was vast in size. – 'as big as the *Queen Mary*' went into the language.

The *Queen Mary* was followed four years later by the *Queen Elizabeth* of 1940 (No. 66) and this ship had the distinction of being the largest passenger liner ever built at a grand total of 83,673 gross tons. A smaller version of the big liners, the second *Mauretania* of 1939 (Nos. 67 and 68), was already in service when the Second World War started.

So again the Cunard fleet went to war and when hostilities ended in 1945 six large Cunarders did not return. In addition, a further three were retained as repair ships by the Royal Navy. The years 1946 to 1948 saw the re-introduction of Cunard liners to the North Atlantic and the two big *Queens*, whose troop-carrying capacities were claimed by Churchill to have clipped two years off the Second World

s.s. "MONGOLIA."
9,505 Tons.   14,000 h.p.

P AND O

Just through all right, only a little late. - Am comfortably fixed up on board & weather looks favourable. - Love to all.   Osborne

6. **Mongolia** *(9,505 tons, P&O) was an intermediate liner built at Greenock in 1903/4 for the Australian mail service. This is a good example of an early Reid postcard.*   *(Andrew Reid & Co. for P&O)*

War, returned to their natural element, maintaining a weekly service between Southampton and New York. They were joined by the fourth big liner in the team, the *Caronia* (No. 69), known as the Green Goddess from the colour of her hull, and then by four smaller intermediate liners of which the *Carmania* (No. 70) was a typical example. By the summer of 1960 Cunard had ten large liners in commission, but by that time the jet passenger aircraft had arrived and was beginning to take large numbers of passengers away from the shipping companies.

The aircraft proved unconquerable. In 1960 alone 70,000 commercial aircraft crossings of the Atlantic were made and by the winter of 1965 the Cunard *Queens* were losing £8,000 each day on the North Atlantic and not much less when cruising. Such economic nonsense could not continue for ever and on 8 May 1967 Cunard announced the withdrawal of both *Queens*. The news produced hardly a ripple in the world's press. Gone were the days when the superliners were never far from the headlines of newspapers in six or seven world capitals.

However, by this time Cunard had commissioned their last superliner, the *Queen Elizabeth 2*, and she still has a short season of scheduled runs on the North Atlantic in summer and so maintains the Cunard tradition which, in 1990, had extended for 150 years

When Cunard took over the White Star Line in 1934 they acquired one of the world's most famous shipping companies. The White Star Line dated back to 1869 when a company known as Oceanic Steam Navigation Co. Ltd. was founded in Liverpool by Thomas Ismay. This was a steamship company and an offshoot of the White Star fleet of sailing clippers. It always traded under the title White Star Line but retained its official name.

Thomas Ismay stands out as the leading British shipowner of the last part of the nineteenth century. His passenger ships were always larger then their predecessors and he traded not only in America but also to Australia and South Africa. After some smaller liners, of which the *Majestic* (No. 71) was the last White Star liner to hold the Blue Riband, Ismay launched the *Oceanic* (Nos. 9 and 72) and then

23

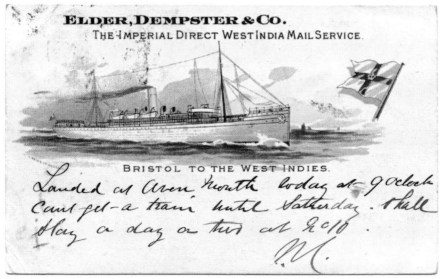

ELDER, DEMPSTER & CO.
THE IMPERIAL DIRECT WEST INDIA MAIL SERVICE

BRISTOL TO THE WEST INDIES.

7. Elder Dempster maintained a Bristol – Caribbean service in the first decade of this century for passengers and bananas! Bristol remained a banana terminal until the 1980s.

(Andrew Reid & Co. for Elder Dempster)

proceeded to an even larger ship, the *Celtic* of 1901 and her sister *Cedric* (Nos 14 and. 73). He died in 1900 and two years later his White Star Line was acquired by the Morgan Combine. Morgan was an American financier who had built up an industrial empire in steel. He became interested in the Atlantic shipping trade as early as 1883 and set out to get a monopoly on the North Atlantic. In addition to the White Star Line, Morgan then acquired the Leyland and Atlantic Transport Line. He also bought heavily into the two large German companies, Hamburg-Amerika and North German Lloyd.

The line built two similar ships to the *Celtic* – the *Baltic* (No. 74) and the *Adriatic* (No. 75). It was about this latter ship that Captain E.J. Smith, who would later command the *Titanic*, made his now notorious statement about ocean liners being 'unsinkable'. The ill-fated Captain Smith never in fact used the term 'unsinkable' about the *Titanic*, but the damage had been done already.

White Star jumped into the headlines on Saturday 23 January, 1909 when their 15,400 ton liner *Republic* (No. 76), outward bound for

the Mediterranean with 400 passengers, ran into fog and collided with an Italian liner, the *Florida*, inward bound with 900 emigrants. As she sliced into the *Republic*, killing three passengers, she also collapsed the radio shack where Marconi operator Jack Binns was sound asleep. All electric power failed but Binns quickly rigged his set to emergency batteries and sent off the first radio distress signal in history from a ship at sea. Other vessels heard the message and groped their way through the fog to find the *Republic* and rescue all her surviving passengers.

Just two months to the day after the accident to the *Republic*, the White Star Line's greatest ship yet was laid down at the Belfast yard of Harland and Wolff. The new monster was the second of three large ships, twice as big as any existing rival, that the White Star Chairman, Bruce Ismay, planned to give his company domination of the North Atlantic passenger services. First of the three ships was the *Olympic* (Nos. 10, 77, 79 and 80) a large four-funnel liner which became a swift favourite with the travelling public.

Grüß vom Bord " *Windhuk* " Lourenzo Marques

With kind regards

8. German East Africa Line card used postally at Lourenzo Marques in April 1906. The ship illustrated is typical of the line's large fleet and could be used on board any vessel.
(Deutsche Ost Afrika official).

The second was to receive a name which haunts the imagination whenever it is mentioned – *Titanic* (Nos. 11, 12 and 78). She was virtually a sister ship of *Olympic* but slightly larger and so at the time that she left Southampton on her maiden voyage for New York on 10 April 1912, she was the largest ship in the world.

The story of the maiden voyage of the *Titanic* has been recorded many times as the most famous wreck in history. She remains the largest ship ever to sink on the high seas in

peace time and her death toll has never been exceeded, except in war years. It is not surprising that, as the years roll by, a forest of sturdy legends have grown up around the ship. The recent deep dive expeditions led by Dr. Robert Ballard have done something to dispel these legends, but the facts are bad enough. In the late evening of 14 April 1912, after ignoring several warnings of ice, and steaming at 22 knots in an ice field, the *Titanic* struck an iceberg and sank two and a half hours later with the loss of 1,503 lives.

9. **Oceanic** *(17,274 tons, White Star Line) came out in 1899 as the largest ship in the world, a record she held until 1901.* *(Artist: Charles Dixon. Publisher: White Star Official)*

After the *Titanic* disaster the White Star Line was never the same again. It still had twenty years or so of life left to it but the memory of the disaster lingered on and there can have been few passengers who stepped aboard a White Star vessel in the succeeding years that did not give the *Titanic* at least a passing thought. More ill-fortune was to follow as the third of the big White Star liners, the *Britannic*, at the time the largest British ship, was lost when she struck a mine in the Gallipoli Campaign on 1 November 1916. Fortunately, the evacuation of the ship was orderly, weather conditions perfect and fatal casualties were limited to twenty-eight as a result. But the White Star Line had lost the second of the great trio of ships planned with such care in the pre-war years.

When the war ended the White Star Line received two large German liners from the German lines as compensation for war damage and also built or acquired several new ships. The first to arrive was *Homeric* (Nos. 17 and 81), the ex-German *Columbus,* and she was followed by the largest ship in the world at the

time, the ex-German *Bismarck* which was renamed *Majestic* and served as the company's flagship (Nos. 82 to 84).

The White Star Line went on through the 1920s in fairly good economic shape, adding such ships as the *Laurentic* (No. 85) and the *Doric* (No. 86). During these years, however, many famous old liners in White Star ownership went for scrap and, after an ill-fated attempt to build a superliner which was abandoned on the stocks, the last pair of White Star liners, the *Georgic* (No. 87) and *Britannic* (No. 88) became the last ships to sail under the White Star flag. In 1934 came the merger with Cunard.

During its long career, the White Star Line collected around it a number of subsidiary companies, particularly during the time of the Morgan Combine. Typical of these were lines like the Red Star Line and the Atlantic Transport Line. Red Star originated as far back as 1872 when a group of American businessmen set up a company based in Philadelphia but with its ships registered in

☆ WHITE STAR LINE R.M.S "OLYMPIC" ☆
COMPARED WITH VARIOUS FAMOUS BUILDINGS.

10. **Olympic** *(45,324 tons) contrasted to the world's largest buildings to boast the size of the latest and largest liners in a card typical of the publisher.* *(White Star Official – composite).*

Belgium. Red Star liners continued to set sail under the Belgian flag throughout the history of the line which lasted until 1935.

In its last years, the company ran few vessels but in the first two decades of this century it owned a very attractive fleet. Typical of these was the *Lapland* (No. 89) which operated between Antwerp and New York from 1909. In the 1920s the *Pennland* (No. 91) and the *Westernland* (No. 92) were attractive Red Star liners and the *Arabic* (No. 90) was chartered from the White Star Line for the last four years of the '20s. The most famous Red Star liner of all was the *Belgenland*, 27,132 tons (No. 93), which pioneered world cruising and was the company's last ship when *Pennland* and *Westernland* were sold to a German buyer together with the line's goodwill in 1935.

The Atlantic Transport Line dated from 1881 and again was taken into the Morgan Combine. It operated intermediate services between London and New York and typical of its ships were the *Minneapolis* (No. 94) and the *Minnesota* (No. 95), which was among the last

of the fleet before it passed out of existence in the early '30s.

No history of North Atlantic liners would be complete without some reference to the Anchor Line of Glasgow. This old company was formed in 1852 by the Glasgow firm of Handyside and Henderson and it had traded very successfully up until 1912 when it was acquired by Cunard who continued to operate it under their guidance, but with the vessels retaining the Anchor Livery and company title.

The Anchor Line is remembered today for a series of very attractive liners which sailed between Glasgow and the American continent. Typical of them in the early years of this century was the *Caledonia* (No. 96) the third ship of the name to serve the line. She was a casualty of the First World War but two more passenger liners called *Caledonia* were later to serve the line. Between the wars the fourth *Caledonia* (No. 98) and her sister ship *Transylvania* (No. 97) were a pair of graceful three-funnel liners, both of which were to end up being lost on war service.

27

The Most Appalling Disaster in Maritime History.
The White Star Liner "TITANIC," sunk on her maiden voyage off Cape Race, 15th April, 1912.

11. **Titanic** *postcards are seldom what they seem. This is a reproduction of a Valentine card issued in the USA in 1972. Examples are common but dealers offer them at up to £15 – £25.*

The Anchor Line continued to operate passenger vessels under its flag until the 1960s when the last of its liners went for scrap. Today the line sails on with a fleet of gas carriers.

During the First World War Cunard found a further subsidiary of the Anchor Line. In 1916 it took over the Donaldson Line, a company that dates back to 1855. When it started operating services between the Clyde and South America, Donaldson liners were quite famous in their day and *Letitia* (No. 99) was typical of their vessels in the first decade of this century. Donaldson Line continued to operate independently and in 1939 owned two large vessels, the second *Letitia* (No. 100) and a ship that will remain famous for the rest of history. This was the *Athenia* (No. 101), the 13,500 ton liner which was the first ship to be lost in the Second World War. The sinking of the *Athenia* led to an international incident of grave proportions because over 100 Americans perished. The big liner was outward bound north of the Irish coast late in the evening of 3 September 1939 when she was torpedoed by a

U-20 and went down very quickly.

Throughout the history of the North Atlantic liner routes, German companies have played an important part. Foremost among these have been North German Lloyd (Norddeutscher Lloyd – NDL) and the Hamburg-Amerika lines. The North German Lloyd was founded in 1857 by an influential merchant from Bremen called H. Meier. Its first steamer was built in Scotland and took its name from its home port of Bremen. The service prospered and by 1887 the Lloyd was running ships to the Caribbean, Brazil and Argentina. A typical German liner of the NDL from the Victorian period is the *Konig Albert* (No. 102).

It was this company's flagship, the brilliant *Kaiser Wilhelm der Grosse* of 1897 that really established the company as a major force in international trade (No. 103). The ship was launched in March 1897 in the presence of the Kaiser and 30,000 wildly cheering Germans. NDL followed her up with four very similar ships in the next eight years. Each was a four stacker and each a little larger and a good deal

12. **Titanic** *again – except that the vessel shown is* Olympic, *her sister ship.* Titanic *had her promenade deck plated in.*

faster. All of them had huge reciprocating engines to get the necessary power and at high speeds there was considerable vibration. *Kaiser Wilhelm II* (No. 104) and *Kronprinz Wilhelm* (No. 105) were two 'Blue Riband' ships but after their experiences of record breaking NDL were content to build slower and more comfortable vessels of which the *Columbus* (No. 106) was a good example when she came out just after the First World War. At 32,000 tons she was among the largest ships in the world and very economic to operate. The *Columbus* was built to replace war losses as the North German Lloyd lost all its ships during the First World War.

After the *Columbus* a number of smaller ships were produced of which the *Dresden* (No. 107) was typical, until the Lloyd dramatically re-entered the race for the Atlantic record in 1929 with the two superliners *Europa* (No. 108) and *Bremen*. These wonderful ships were prominent on the North Atlantic right up to the outbreak of war in 1939. They held the record from 1929 to 1933 when the Italians wrested

the crown from them.

The *Bremen* was destroyed by fire during the war, while the *Europa* was ceded to France in 1945 to become the *Liberté*. Once again the North German Lloyd was obliged to rebuild a passenger fleet. This it did by using old Swedish tonnage and the *Berlin* (No. 109) became its first liner after the war. In 1971 North German Lloyd amalgamated with Hamburg-Amerika.

The name of the Hamburg-Amerika Line will always be linked with that of Albert Ballin who became chairman of the company in 1880. The Hamburg-Amerika Line dates back to 1847 but it was under Ballin that it achieved its greatest fame. More than any other shipowner, he foresaw the possibilities of taking luxury to sea, and he was the first magnate to employ specialist interior decorators, and chefs de cuisine aboard his ships. He enjoyed the personal friendship of the Emperor Wilhelm II and obtained much political support from him.

He began to build large Atlantic liners in 1887 as a direct reply to the North German

13. **Campania** *(12,950 tons, Cunard) and her sister* Lucania *were Cunard's flagships in the naughty nineties. Their luxury fittings show up well in this card, posted in* Ivernia *in 1907.*

Lloyd and by 1890 owned one of the largest passenger services in the world. It was then that he produced the *Deutschland* (No. 110) and although she took the Atlantic record her indifferent success convinced Ballin that passengers would be attracted far more by luxury than they would by speed. So *Deutschland* was the only record breaker that the line owned. Instead Ballin turned to great size and his three big liners which emerged just before the First World War were the largest ships in the world, comfortable and safe. The result of the First World War meant that all three ended up in the hands of Germany's enemies and other people (Ballin had died in 1918) were left to rebuild the line's fortunes. Between wars they produced four large ships, of which *Hamburg* (No. 111) was typical, and these four operated a very successful transatlantic service.

The United States of America has never been noted as an operator of passenger liners although such companies as the American Line did operate before the First World War. One of

their later ships was the *Philadelphia* (No. 112) which first appeared as the Inman liner *City of Paris* of 1889.

After the war, the United States Government found itself with a large fleet of old German liners on its hands. The ships were under the control of the United States Shipping Board Estate Agency and it was obvious that no private owner had the funds available to bring such a vast collection of ageing liners into commercial service. In any other country they would have been quietly sent away for scrap. With a large vote of funds from Congress, United States Lines was founded which took over a number of the larger liners including the vast *Leviathan* (No. 113). This ship had been built in 1914 as the *Vaterland* for the Hamburg-Amerika Line.

Operating under American law, the *Leviathan* was almost impossible to fill and never made a profit. The reasons were not hard to find. These were the Prohibition years in the United States and the provisions of the Prohibition Act extended to American ships at

14. **Cedric** *(21,035 tons, White Star) outward bound in a fine study by Charles Dixon. One of the 'big four', she sailed from 1903 to 1932.* *(Artist: Charles Dixon. Publisher: White Star)*

15. **Carmania** *(20,000 tons, Cunard) was Cunard's first turbine propelled liner. The card is from the famous OILETTE Series 'Celebrated Liners' – No. 9268* *(Tuck OILETTE No. 9268)*

16. *Union Castle official card showing* **Edinburgh Castle.** *(Artist: Maurice Rendell. Publisher: Union Castle)*

A UNION-CASTLE LINER SIGNALLING "ALL'S WELL."

sea. Even foreign vessels had to padlock their bar stores at the twelve mile limit. Then in the mid-'20s the United States Emigration Laws restricted entry into the country and further losses followed. The *Levi*athan was withdrawn in the early '30s but she was replaced by two smaller and profitable liners, *Manhattan* and *Washington* (No. 114). These ships became very popular specially after the end of Prohibition. This allowed the United States Lines to continue and, after the war, they received a 48 million dollar subsidy in 1950 to produce the *United States* (No. 115), a 50,000

ton superliner which smashed the Atlantic record in 1952 at 35.39 knots average. It is unlikely that this record will ever be broken by a conventional steamship.

Not far behind the German and British lines in prominence was the great French company, the CGT. Known to travellers in Britain and the United States as the French Line, it had been founded in 1855 and throughout its career received much support from the French Government, which was concerned for the weakness of French merchant shipping. After the First World War the French Line introduced

32

17. **Homeric** *(34,351 tons, White Star). The big ex-German* Columbus *shows up well in a typical White Star card from the 1920s.* *(Artist: William McDowell. Publisher: White Star)*

one of the all time favourites of the North Atlantic, the *Ile de France* (No. 116), a large vessel with three funnels. She was a magnificent ship and gained a deserved reputation for excellence. Veteran travellers were prepared to wait a week in order to travel on her and her name found its way even into the popular songs of the day.

The crowning achievement of this great line came in the mid-1930s when the famous Blue Riband, *Normandie,* second only in size to the *Queen Elizabeth,* was possibly the most outstanding passenger liner ever put into service (No. 117). The *Normandie* possessed many innovations and her tragic loss by accidental fire in 1942 must be rated among the great social and economic disasters of our time.

Another line prominent on the North Atlantic in the 1930s was the Italia Line, the state organised company created by the dictator, Mussolini. In 1932 this company produced the *Rex* (No. 118) which was Italy's largest ever passenger ship and the only holder of the Blue Riband from 1933 to 1935. In company with her sister, the slightly smaller *Conte di Savoia,*

the *Rex* was among the finest liners operating between the wars. She was destroyed in an air attack in the Adriatic in 1944.

Two nations that were prominent on the North Atlantic during the period of ocean liners were Holland and Sweden. The Dutch company Holland-America Line was founded in 1855 in Rotterdam and established a record for quality of service which remains to this day. In the pre-war years they ran a series of small liners such as *Volendam* (No. 119), while also running the 30,000 ton *Statendam* (No. 120), a three-funnel monster, which was their flagship until she was destroyed in the German attack on Rotterdam in 1940.

Today the Atlantic liner as a passenger commuter business has all but disappeared. Apart from Cunard's *QE2* and her annual summer season of transatlantic crossings, which are largely cruises, the main concentration of passengers enjoy sunshine and high life on a round the year basis. So large ships continue to be built and the romance of the liner continues.

33

18. **Andania** *(13,950 tons, Cunard). A strong whiff of 'Art Deco' appears in this 1930s card of a Cunard intermediate liner.* *(Artist: Sam J.M. Brown. Publisher: Thomas Forman)*

19. **Southern Cross** *(20,204 tons, Shaw, Savill). A commercial card of the innovative* Southern Cross *of 1955.* *(Artist: John Nicholson. Publisher: Salmon)*

20. **Laos** *(13,212 tons, Messageries Maritime). An attractive study in the French style of one of four similar ships for the Europe – Far East trade.*
(Artist: Roger Chapelet. Publisher: Messageries Maritime)

21. **Umbria** *(8,128 tons, Cunard) was Cunard's last ship to carry auxiliary sail and their last single screw record breaker.* *(Artist: Charles Dixon. Publisher: Cunard)*

22. **Etruria** *(8,120 tons, Cunard) actually set her auxiliary sails in 1902 when she lost her single propeller. She was eventually towed to the Azores.* *(Artist: Charles Dixon. Publisher: Cunard)*

23. **Campania** *(12,950 tons, Cunard) completed 500 round voyages in a long career which ended with her conversion into an early RN aircraft carrier.* *(Publisher: Turner & Dunnett)*

24. **Campania** *in Queenstown (Cobh) Harbour while tenders bring out passengers, probably emigrants to the New World.* *(Artist: Charles Dixon. Publisher: Cunard)*

25. **Caronia** *(19,687 tons, Cunard) carried reciprocating engines as opposed to turbines in* Carmania. *The artist's taste for sunsets dominates this card.*
(Artist: Odin Rosenvinge. Publisher: Taylor, Garnett, Evans & Co.)

37

26. **Carmania** *looking just as a Cunarder should to proud Englishmen of the 1920s.*
(Artist: Charles Dixon. Publisher: Taylor, Garnett, Evans & Co.)

27. **Carmania** *in another style, painted in her last years.*
(Artist: Sam J.M. Brown. Publisher: Thomas Forman)

28. **Carmania** *yet again. An 'Art Deco' card from Rosenvinge in a series that did not prove popular.*
(Artist: Odin Rosenvinge. Publisher: Turner & Dunnett)

29. **Lusitania** *(31,550 tons, Cunard). The tragic record breaker depicted in a Sam Brown picture for*
Tuck's OILETTE Series No. 9268. This card predates the wreck.
(Artist: Sam J.M. Brown. Publisher: Tuck OILETTE No. 9268)

30. **Mauretania** *(31,938 tons, Cunard). The most famous liner of all time which held the Atlantic record for twenty-two years between 1909 and 1929. The card carries an identical number to No. 29).*
(Tuck OILETTE No. 9268)

31. **Mauretania.** Mauretania's *elegance shows well in Rosenvinge's famous study which was even used for jigsaw puzzles. Another hand has mis-spelt her name!*
(Artist: Odin Rosenvinge. Publisher: Turner & Dunnett)

32. **Saxonia** *(14,281 tons, Cunard) had the tallest funnel (106ft. – 32.31m) ever fitted to a liner. This card is an early Shoesmith, showing a very different style from his later work.*
(Artist: K.D. Shoesmith. Publisher: Turner & Dunnett)

33. **Ivernia** *(14,067 tons, Cunard) possessed the same tall funnel as* Saxonia *(106ft. – 32.31m). She was torpedoed on New Year's Day 1917 off Cape Matapan by UB-47, which had been sent overland in sections to the Mediterranean.* *(Artist: Charles Dixon. Publisher: Turner & Dunnett)*

41

34. **Carpathia** *(13,603 tons, Cunard) earned immortality as the ship that rescued* Titanic's *survivors. She met her own violent end at the hands of a U-boat off Bishop Rock in July 1918.*
(Artist: Sam J.M. Brown. Publisher: Turner & Dunnett)

35. **Franconia (1)** *(18,150 tons, Cunard). A short-lived Cunarder (1911-1916) which operated Liverpool – Boston services and sailed New York to the Mediterranean in winter.*
(Artist: Sam J.M. Brown. Publisher: Turner & Dunnett)

36. **Aquitania** *(45,647 tons, Cunard). The first of Cunard's safer liners,* Aquitania *served thirty-six years in all proving very popular. She was the last 'four stacker'.* *(Tuck OILETTE No. 8690)*

37. **Aquitania** *leaving New York in an unusual sea and landscape from Odin Rosenvinge.*
(Artist: Odin Rosenvinge. Publisher: Turner & Dunnett)

38. **Aquitania** *in a more impressionistic style from Frank Mason in the Cunard set dating from 1929.*
(Artist: Frank Mason. Publisher: Thomas Forman)

39. **Berengaria** *(52,226 tons, Cunard) was the big ex-German* Imperator *which Cunard bought in 1920 and which served as flagship until* Queen Mary *arrived in 1936.*
(Artist: Frank Mason. Publisher: Thomas Forman)

CUNARD LINE   R.M.S. "BERENGARIA"   GROSS TONNAGE 52,700

40. **Berengaria** *in typical Rosenvinge 'rose glow' style.*
(Artist: Odin Rosenvinge. Publisher: Thomas Forman)

CUNARD LINE   R.M.S. "BERENGARIA"   TONNAGE 52,300

41. **Berengaria** *again, this time in more massive shape (as she was) from the softer brush of Sam Brown.*
(Artist: Sam J.M. Brown. Publisher: Thomas Forman)

45

THE NEW CUNARDER "ALBANIA."

42. **Albania (2)** *(12,767 tons, Cunard). Largely a cargo carrier,* Albania *was not a success in Cunard service and was sold to Italian owners after only four years service.*
(Artist: Walter Thomas. Publisher: Turner & Dunnett)

CUNARD LINE   R.M.S. "SAMARIA"   GROSS TONNAGE 20,000

43. **Samaria (2)** *(19,597 tons, Cunard). Built to replace war losses.* Samaria *came into service in 1922 on the Liverpool – Boston service.*   *(Artist: Odin Rosenvinge. Publisher: Turner & Dunnett)*

CUNARD LINE   R.M.S. "SCYTHIA"   TONNAGE 20.000

44. **Scythia (2)** *(19,930 tons, Cunard) was* Samaria's *sister and lasted until 1958. She was typical of an inter-wars Cunarder.* *(Artist: Sam J.M. Brown. Publisher: Thomas Forman)*

45. **Scythia** *in post-World War Two guise on the Canadian service. The card has been 'doctored' to delete the New York skyline from* Laconia *(No. 46.)* *(Artist: K.D. Shoesmith. Publisher: Thomas Forman)*

47

46. **Laconia** *(16,695 tons, Cunard). A repeat of* Samaria *and* Scythia, Laconia *fell victim to U-156 in September 1942. Subsequent events caused Admiral Donitz to issue his infamous* Laconia *order.*
(Artist: K.D. Shoesmith. Publisher: Thomas Forman)

47. **Laconia** *in a Walter Thomas sketch which shows clearly the influence of Rosenvinge.*
(Artist: Walter Thomas. Publisher: Turner & Dunnett)

THE NEW CUNARDER "ANDANIA 14,000 TONS

48. **Andania** *(13,950 tons, Cunard). The first of six small liners built for Cunard from 1922 onwards. She was lost in World War Two.* *(Artist: Odin Rosenvinge. Publisher: Turner & Dunnett)*

CUNARD LINE   R.M.S. AURANIA   TONNAGE 14,000

49. **Aurania** *(13,984 tons, Cunard). Another of the 'A' class.* *(Artist: C.E. Turner. Publisher: Taylor, Garnett & Evans)*

50. **Ascania** *(14,013 tons, Cunard) was the last of the six 'A' class liners, seen here in a 1934 picture off the Liverpool Bar Lightship.* *(Artist: Sam J.M. Brown. Publisher: Thomas Forman)*

51. **Alaunia** *(14,030 tons, Cunard) ended her days as a Royal Navy Leary repair ship.* *(Artist: C.E. Turner. Publisher: Taylor, Garnett, Evans & Co.)*

52. **Lancastria** *(16,243 tons, Cunard) came out as* Tyrrhenia *in 1922, an unsuitable name even for Cunard. In 1924, she became* Lancastria. *Her loss by air bombing at St. Nazaire in June 1940 caused 3,000 deaths.* *(Artist: K.D. Shoesmith. Publisher: Thomas Forman)*

53. **Franconia (2)** *(20,175 tons, Cunard). Painted here in cruising white under Mediterranean skies, but see No. 54.* *(Artist: K.D. Shoesmith. Publisher: Thomas Forman)*

54. **Franconia (2)** *in the same basic painting by Shoesmith, but converted to North Atlantic colours. This card was printed post-war, after Shoesmith's death in 1939.*

(Artist: K.D. Shoesmith. Publisher: Thomas Forman)

55. **Franconia (2)** *in Rosenvinge orange glow.*

(Artist: Odin Rosenvinge. Publisher: Turner & Dunnett)

Nos. 56 to 63 are taken from Charles Turner's vertical series of the Cunard fleet of the 1920s.
(Artist: C.E. Turner. Publisher: Taylor, Garnett, Evans & Co.)

57. Mauretania

(31,938 tons, Cunard)

56. Carmania

(19,524 tons, Cunard).

CUNARD R.M.S. BERENGARIA

TONNAGE 52,300

59. **Berengaria** *(52,226 tons, Cunard).*

CUNARD R.M.S. AQUITANIA

TONNAGE 45,650

58. **Aquitania** *(45,647 tons, Cunard).*

61. **Samaria** *(19,597 tons, Cunard).*

60. **Scythia** *(19,930 tons, Cunard).*

CUNARD R.M.S. AURANIA · TONNAGE 14,000

63. **Aurania** *(13,984 tons, Cunard)*

CUNARD R.M.S. LACONIA · TONNAGE 20,000

62. **Laconia** *(19,695 tons, Cunard).*

CUNARD LINE R.M.S. "CARINTHIA."
TONNAGE 20,000. LENGTH 624 FEET. BREADTH 74 FEET.

64. **Carinthia (2)** *(20,277 tons, Cunard). A rare vertical card from Rosenvinge of the popular Cunarder, lost in June 1940 to U-boat attack.*
(Artist: Odin Rosenvinge. Publisher: Turner & Dunnett)

65. **Queen Mary** *(81,235tons, Cunard) at speed in a picture used for cards, menus, programmes and souvenir pottery.* *(Artist: C.E. Turner. Publisher: Thomas Forman)*

66. **Queen Elizabeth** *(83,673 tons, Cunard) in the companion card to No. 65 which was used by Cunard for similar purposes.* *(Artist: C.E. Turner. Publisher: Thomas Forman)*

Cunard White Star   The New " Mauretania "

67. **Mauretania (2)** *(35,739 tons, Cunard). A pre-launch card issued in 1938. The card advertised the 1939 New York World Fair.*   *(Artist: C.F. Hopkinson. Publisher: Thomas Forman)*

Cunard "Mauretania"

68. **Mauretania (2)** *in the last years of her career, painted in 'cruising' green. She was scrapped in 1966.*
(Artist: C.E. Turner. Publisher: Thomas Forman)

69. **Caronia (2)** *(34,183 tons, Cunard). The great 'Green Goddess' spent most of her career cruising, occasionally acting as relief ship on the North Atlantic.*
(Artist: C.E. Turner. Publisher: Thomas Forman)

70. **Carmania (2)** *(22,592 tons, Cunard) was the re-named* Saxonia *of 1954. Here she is seen in green livery before her sale to Russia in 1971. She sails today as* Leonid Sobinov.
(Artist: C.E. Turner. Publisher: Thomas Forman)

71. **Majestic** *(9,965 tons, White Star) and her sister* Teutonic *both held the Blue Riband in the 1890s.*
(Artist: Charles Dixon. Publisher: White Star)

72. **Oceanic** *(17,274 tons, White Star). The largest liner in the world when launched in 1899, the* beautiful Oceanic *was wrecked in the Shetlands in 1914.*
(Artist:C.M. Pridday. Publisher: Tuck OILETTE No.6228)

73. **Cedric** *(21,035 tons, White Star). One of White Star's 'Big Four', they deliberately put comfort before speed and were known as the '7-day boats'.*
(Artist: Charles Dixon. Publisher: White Star Official)

74. **Baltic** *(23,876 tons, White Star). Another of the 'Big Four', she served for thirty years until 1932.*
(Artist: Montague B. Black. Publisher: White Star)

75. **Adriatic** *(24,679 tons, White Star) was the ship that Captain Smith (later of* Titanic) *called unsinkable. He never used the word to describe the* Titanic.
(Artist: Montague B. Black. Publisher: White Star)

76. **Republic** *(15,378 tons, White Star). While serving on the New York – Mediterranean service in* January 1909, Republic *collided with the Italian* Florida *near the Nortucket lightship. Wireless was used to summon help for the first time.* Republic *sank.* *(Artist: Charles Dixon. Publisher: White Star)*

77. **Olympic** (45,234 tons, White Star). An early card of the big liner. Compare this with No. 78. *(Tuck OILETTE No. 9898)*

78. **Titanic** (46,329 tons, White Star). The artwork of this card is identical to No. 77, only the title being overprinted. The card dates from December 1913, posted in Seymour, Wisconsin).
(Tuck OILETTE No. 9898)

79. **Olympic** *on a 'summery' day in the English Channel.*
(Artist: Walter Thomas. Publisher: White Star)

80. **Olympic** *awaits the pilot. Versions of this card exist overprinted 'Cunard White Star' after the lines merged in 1934.* *(Artist: Sam J.M. Brown. Publisher: White Star)*

81. **Homeric** *(34,351 tons, White Star). Launched as* Columbus *for NDL,* Homeric *was a war prize and spent her latter years cruising. This card was posted from Majorca.*
(Artist: Walter Thomas. Publisher: White Star)

82. **Majestic** *(56,551 tons, White Star) was the largest ship in the world from 1914 until overtaken by* Normandie *in 1935.* *(Publisher: White Star)*

83. **Majestic** *in New York's Hudson River. The card is unsigned but the style appears to be McDowell's.*
(White Star)

84. **Majestic** *after the merger with Cunard in 1934. Her last commercial voyage was in 1936 but she burnt out in 1939 while in use as a static training ship.*
(Artist: Walter Thomas. Publisher: White Star)

85. **Laurentic (2)** *(18,724 tons, White Star) cruising at Barcelona. The card was used partially in 1931.*
(Artist: Walter Thomas. Publisher: White Star)

86. **Doric** *(16,484 tons, White Star). This short-lived liner served only ten years and was scrapped after a collision in 1935.* *(Artist: W. McDowell. Publisher: White Star)*

87. **Georgic** *(27,759 tons, White Star). The last ship to be built for the White Star Line.*
(Artist: Sam J.M. Brown. Publisher: White Star)

88. **Britannic** *(26,943 tons, White Star) sailed in White Star colours throughout her career which lasted until 1960.*
(Artist: W. McDowell. Publisher: White Star)

89. **Lapland** *(18,694 tons, Red Star) operated between Antwerp and New York from 1909.*
(Artist: Charles Dixon. Publisher: Official)

90. **Arabic** *(16,786 tons, White Star) was NDL Berlin until 1919. She was chartered to Red Star between 1926 and 1930.*
(Artist: Charles Dixon. Publisher: Official)

71

RED STAR
LINE.

TRIPLE-SCREW "PENNLAND"
(EX-PITTSBURGH)
16.332 TONS.

91. **Pennland** *(16,322 tons, Red Star) began life as* Pittsburgh *for the American Line, then joined White Star, Red Star and Holland-America. The card was posted in 1918 in New York.*
(Artist: Charles Dixon. Official0

92. **Westernland** *(16,313 tons, Red Star) was built for the Dominion Line as* Regina *and then followed* Pennland *as a pair.* *(Artist: Charles Dixon, Official)*

93. **Belgenland** *(27,132 tons, Red Star) was by far the largest Red Star liner. She pioneered world cruising and is seen here at Port Said.* *(Artist: Charles Dixon, Official)*

73

94. **Minneapolis** *(13,448 tons, Atlantic Transport) sailed between London and New York from 1900. She was lost in World War One.* *(Tuck OILETTE No. 9126)*

95. **Minnesota** *(11,667 tons, Atlantic Transport) used this name only from 1927 until her scrapping in 1929. Previously she was* Zeeland *(Red Star) and* Northland *(Dominion).*

(Artist: Charles Dixon, Official)

ANCHOR LINE.—Twin-Screw Steamship "CALEDONIA."

96. **Caledonia (3)** *(9,223 tons, Anchor Line). On Glasgow – New York service, the third* Caledonia *was a casualty of World War One.* *(Anchor Official)*

ANCHOR LINE—T.S.S. "TRANSYLVANIA"

97. **Transylvania (2)** *(16,923 tons, Anchor). One of a pair of graceful three-stackers, She was torpedoed in August 1940 and lost while on war service.* *(Anchor Official)*

ANCHOR LINE—T.S.S. "CALEDONIA"

98. **Caledonia (4)** *(17,046 tons, Anchor), the sister of* Transylvania, *was also a war loss.*
(Anchor Official)

H.M.H.S. "LETITIA" — of Donaldson Line.

99. **Letitia (1)** *(8,991 tons, Donaldson). A wartime card of* Letitia *as a hospital ship, a role in which she was wrecked on 1 August 1917 at Halifax, Nova Scotia.* *(Donaldson Official)*

ANCHOR-DONALDSON LINE—TURBINE TWIN-SCREW STEAMSHIP "LETITIA."

100. **Letitia (2)** *(13,475 tons, Anchor Donaldson) was renamed* Captain Cook *in 1952 when used to carry emigrants to Australia.* *(Artist: Odin Rosenvinge. Publisher: Turner & Dunnett)*

DONALDSON-ATLANTIC LINE—TURBINE TWIN-SCREW STEAMSHIP "ATHENIA."

101. **Athenia** *(13,465 tons, Anchor Donaldson) in the St. Lawrence at Quebec. She became notorious as the first ship to be torpedoed (3 September 1939) in World War Two* *(Artist: Walter Thomas. Publisher: Turner & Dunnett)*

102. **Konig Albert** *(10,643 tons, NDL) dates from 1899 and sailed to the Far East before transfer to the New York run.* *(Tuck OILETTE No. 9124)*

103. **Kaiser Wilhelm der Grosse** *(14,349 tons, NDL) was the first of the German record breakers and took much trade from Cunard.* *(No provenance)*

Twin-screw Express S. S. „Kaiser Wilhelm II" passing the Statue of Liberty.

104. **Kaiser Wilhelm II** *(19,361 tons, NDL) took the Atlantic record in 1904. She was seized as a war prize in the USA in 1917).* *(W. Sander und Sohn, Geestemunde)*

105. *Kronprinz Wilhelm (14,908 tons, NDL) was the second of the NDL four-stack fliers but this ship is her close sister* **Kaiser Wilhelm der Grosse**. *(Tuck OILETTE No. 9124)*

79

106. **Columbus** *(34,351 tons, NDL) as she appeared before her funnels were shortened in 1929 to match* Bremen *and* Europa. *(NDL Official)*

107. **Dresden (2)** *(14,588 tons, NDL) seen off the Needles, I.O.W. She was wrecked in Norway in June 1934.* *(NDL Official)*

108. **Europa** *(46,746 tons, NDL). The greatest liner shown at speed. After World War Two she became CGT's* Liberté. *(NDL Official)*

109. **Berlin** *(18,600 tons, NDL). In 1954 NDL resumed Atlantic services by using the old (1924) Swedish liner* Gripsholm *renamed* Berlin.

110. **Deutschland** *(16,502 tons, Hamburg-Amerika). Hapag's only record breaker convinced Company Chairman, Albert Ballin, that the cost of speed was excessive.* *(Tuck OILETTE No. 9125)*

111. **Hamburg** *(21,455 tons, Hamburg-Amerika) and her sister New York, with two similar, ships operated the Company's Hamburg – New York service between the wars. Post-war, she became a Soviet whaling factory.* *(Hapag Official)*

112. **Philadelphia** *(10,499 tons, American Line) was built with three funnels as Inman Line's* City of Paris *of 1889. As* Paris *she ran aground on the Manacles off Cornwall in 1899 and emerged from refit with two funnels and called* Philadelphia. *(Tuck OILETTE No. 9140)*

113. **Leviathan** *(59,597 tons, United States Lines) was marketed as the 'largest ship in the world' when she was not. Ex-Hapag* Vaterland, *she was never a commercial success.*
(Artist: John H. Fry. Publisher: Salmon)

114. **Washington** *(24,289 tons, United States Lines) and her sister* Manhattan *operated a successful New York – Southampton – Hamburg service in the 1930s.* *(USL Official)*

115. **United States** *(53,329 tons, United States Lines) smashed the Atlantic record in 1952 at 35.39 knots average. It is a speed unlikely to be beaten by a conventional ship.* *(Salmon)*

116. **Ile de France** *(43,153 tons, CGT). The ship that brought 'chic' to the North Atlantic, the* Ile *was a great favourite throughout her career.*
(Artist: Marchard L. Lachotte. Publisher: Tuck OILETTE No. 3592)

117. **Normandie** *(83,423 tons, CGT). Cards of the great French liner are rare. This English version dates from 1941.* *(Artist: Bernard W. Church. Publisher: Salmon)*

118. **Rex** *(51,062 tons, Italia) was Italy's largest ever passenger ship and her only holder of the Blue Riband, from 1933 to 1935.* *(Italia Official)*

119. **Volendam** *(15,434 tons, Holland-America). Built at Harland and Wolff's Govan Yard,* Volendam *survived a torpedo hit in mid-Atlantic in 1940.* *(Artist: Charles Dixon. Publisher: Lankhout for HAL)*

HOLLAND-AMERICA LINE.   ROTTERDAM-NEW YORK

T.S.S. STATENDAM. 30000 Tons Register - 40000 Tons Displacement.

120. **Statendam** *(29,511 tons, Holland-America). Built in Belfast, but fitted out in Rotterdam, the* Statendam *was popular for her quality service. She was burnt out in May 1940 during the German invasion of Holland.* *(Artist: Charles Dixon. Publisher: Lankhout for HAL)*

CHAPTER 4

The Canadian Routes

Although the major share of passenger trade between Europe and the American continent passed through the United States' ports, there has always been a sizeable traffic between Europe and Canada and this chapter deals with the shipping companies that have handled the passenger trade over the years.

Among the most prominent was the Allan Line of Liverpool, famous in its day but now extinct. The Allan Line was formed in Glasgow in 1854 for involvement in the Canadian trade and it experienced many of the misfortunes associated with trading down the St. Lawrence River to Montreal. Between 1857 and 1865, due to insufficient navigation lights, ice and frequent fog, the line lost nine ships and a total of 650 lives. Despite the competition from the Dominion Line and the Beaver Line, Sir Hugh Allan persevered and by the turn of the turn of the century his company was well established.

Always progressive, the Allan Line had been first with steel ships in 1879 and now as the twentieth century dawned it was the first to have turbine driven liners. With a sea speed of 18 knots and space for 1,650 passengers the Allan Line's *Victorian* (No. 122) and *Virginian* (Nos. 121 and 123) were the first large turbine driven steamers on the North Atlantic. Sir Hugh Allan followed these two successful ships with the *Alsatian,* 18,500 tons (No. 124) and this ship was the first large liner to take on a modern appearance of the so-called cruiser stern.

In the first decade of the century the Allan Line began to feel the competition of the Canadian Pacific Railway and its subsidiary company, Canadian Pacific Steamships Limited. The first continental railway from Montreal reached the Pacific coast in July 1886 and the directors of the railway were immediately interested in a steamship line to trade across the Pacific to Yokohama. This

service required fast vessels of considerable size and to build them government aid was needed. This came in 1889 in the shape of a mail contract from the British and Canadian authorities and three fast steamers were promptly ordered from Vickers at Barrow. These were the first of the famous *Empresses* whose white hulls and buff funnels were a familiar sight on both the North Pacific and Atlantic Oceans until the Second World War. At the start of the service a through ticket from Liverpool to Yokohama cost £68 in 1891 although the North Atlantic leg was operated by White Star Line.

It was not until 1903 that the Canadian Pacific started an Atlantic service of its own and this it did by buying up the Beaver Line. Canadian Pacific added the first Atlantic *Empresses,* the *Empress of Britain* and the *Empress of Ireland* (No. 125), 14,000 ton ships which came out in 1906.

The *Empress of Ireland* is famous for her loss in a collision in fog in the St. Lawrence River when she went down in twenty minutes with a death toll of 1,012 lives. The *Empress* had left Quebec for Liverpool on the afternoon of 28 May 1914. Her passenger list did not contain the famous and privileged names that were commonplace on the New York run. The ship was under the command of Captain Kendall – the captor of the notorious murderer Dr. Crippen. That evening in fog the ship collided with a small Norwegian freighter called *Storstad.* She was carrying 10,000 tons of coal and punched a hole in the *Empress* on the waterline. The liner went down as fast as any ship on record. In less than fifteen minutes it was all over and the world had another tragedy with which to cope. Perhaps the outbreak of war three months later and huge casualty list from armies on both sides of the

88

121. **Drottningholm** *(10,754 tons, Swedish America) was the ex-Allan Line* Virginian *sold to Sweden in 1920. She was in turn sold to Horne Lines in 1945.* *(Gotheborg Litho AB)*

122 . **Victorian** *(10,635 tons, Allan Line) was the first large turbine-driven steamer on the North Atlantic and became Canadian Pacific's* Marloch *in 1922.* *(Tuck OILETTE No. 9213)*

ALLAN R.M. LINE, "VICTORIAN" AND "VIRGINIAN," TURBINE TRIPLE-SCREWS, 10,000, TONS

123. **Virginian** *(10,754 tons, Allan Line) was not retained by Canadian Pacific when that company bought Allan Line in 1920.* *(Artist: Odin Rosenvinge. Publisher: Turner & Dunnett)*

Western Front prevented the loss of the *Empress of Ireland* assuming the legendary proportions of the *Titanic.*

After the First World War, Canadian Pacific continued to run successfully on both oceans. The Allan Line had been bought in 1915 and a number of ex-German ships were also added to the fleet. Such vessels as *Melita, Marglen* and *Montlaurier* (Nos. 126 to 128) and various *Empresses,* such as the *Empress of Scotland* and the *Empress of Canada* (Nos. 129 and 130), were all popular ships in their day. The big *Empress of Britain* built in 1931 was lost in World War Two and the conflict brought havoc to the Canadian Pacific Fleet. It did not return to the North Pacific when peace was restored in 1945 as all its vessels except the second *Empress of Scotland* (No. 132) were lost. She was transferred to the North Atlantic and eventually sold to German buyers in 1958 while replacements such as the *Empress of England* (No. 131), smaller but more economic, were placed on the North Atlantic routes.

The building of the Canadian Northern Railway, which first entered into business in 1901, led to its establishment as Canada's second big railway company. The Canadian Northern Railway followed its great competitor into the ship-owning business and in August 1909 it announced the purchase of two liners from the short-lived Egyptian Rail Steamship Company. These ships were called *Cairo* and *Heliopolis.* Now they would be renamed *Royal Edward* (Nos. 133 and 136) and *Royal George* (Nos. 134 and 135) respectively. After a careful look at facilities at Southampton, it was something of a surprise to shipping circles that the British terminal of the line would be Avonmouth, just outside Bristol.

The ships were refitted to passenger liner standards for the North Atlantic and equipped with high standards of facilities (Nos. 134 and 135). The service was opened by the *Royal Edward* on 12 May 1910 when she left Avonmouth for Quebec and Montreal with 750 passengers on board. The *Royal George* followed a fortnight later and the ships

Quadruple-Screw Turbine Steamers "ALSATIAN" & "CALGARIAN," 18,000 Tons.

124. **Alsatian** *(18,481 tons, Allan Line) and her sister* Calgarian *were the first large liners with 'cruiser' sterns. She became Canadian Pacific's* Empress of France.
(Artist: Odin Rosenvinge. Publisher: Turner & Dunnett)

operated that summer until the St. Lawrence River froze over when the service was transferred in the winter months to Halifax and Nova Scotia.

These two steamers maintained an annual service to Canada right up to the outbreak of the First World War when the service was suspended and never restarted when the war ended. By that time *Royal Edward* had been sunk by a German submarine in the Mediterranean in 1915 with very heavy loss of life.

Royal George was eventually acquired by Cunard, which had taken over the Canadian Northern fleet in 1916. At the end of the war, Cunard was desperate for passenger tonnage, having lost twenty-two ships of its fleet to enemy action. *Royal George* was put on the New York service and sailed from Liverpool on her first post-war voyage on 8 February 1919. It should be recalled that *Royal Edward* and *Royal George* had originally been built for the warmer and more kindly seas of the Mediterranean, and Cunard veterans were scathing about the performance of the *George* in the inevitable

February gales. The nickname 'Rolling George' was among the more complementary epithets employed by her exasperated officers and crew. She lasted just a year on the route until the big ex-German liner *Imperator*, soon to become *Berengaria* (see Nos. 39 to 41), came into Cunard service. Then she became a depot ship at Cherbourg but was eventually laid up at Falmouth and broken up in Germany in 1922.

The Canadian routes attracted over the years a number of smaller operators, among whom were Manchester Liners Limited. Established in 1898 by Sir Christopher Furness to run a liner service between Manchester and Canada, the line commenced operations with three small steamers of moderate speed. Although the service was very largely a freight operation, a very high standard of accommodation was provided for a number of passengers. As the line's ships grew in size, it became necessary to provide them with collapsible funnels and masts in order to allow passage under the bridges of the Manchester Ship Canal. All the company's vessels carried names with the

125. **Empress of Ireland** *(14,191 tons, Canadian Pacific) is notorious for her tragic loss in a collision in the St. Lawrence on 30 May 1914. 1,012 people drowned, the ship sinking in fifteen minutes.* *(Tuck OILETTE No. 9682)*

prefix 'Manchester' and the vessel shown in No. 137 is *Manchester Regiment,* a ship absolutely typical of the company's vessels.

However, despite the operations of other companies, the lion's share of the Canadian trade in the early years of this century belonged to White Star and Cunard.

The red burgee of the White Star Line was first seen in the St. Lawrence ports as late as 1909 but the origins of the service date back to

1872 when in May of that year, the *Mississippi,* 2,159 tons, opened the Quebec and Montreal service of the Dominion Line from Liverpool. The Dominion Line was the brainchild of the directors of the Liverpool and Mississippi Steamship Company which had been formed two years previously to exploit the growing cotton trade between the ports of the Gulf of Mexico and the Lancashire cotton mills that operated in the hinterland of Liverpool.

126. **Melita** *(13,967 tons, Canadian Pacific). Ordered for Hapag in 1914,* Melita *was completed for CPR in 1917. She became the Italian* Liguria *in 1935 and was scuttled at Tobruk in 1941.*
(Artist: Oswald F. Pennington. Publisher: CPR Sales)

127. **Marglen** *(10,417 tons, Canadian Pacific) was built in 1898 for Holland-America as* Statendam *and became Allan Line's* Scotian *in 1911. Named* Marglen *in 1922, she was scrapped in 1927.*
(Artist: Oswald F. Pennington. Publisher: CPR Sales)

128. **Montlaurier** *(17,282 tons, Canadian Pacific). Built as* Prinz Phratric Wilhelm *for NDL in 1907, Montlaurier had seven changes of name in her career.*
(Artist: Oswald F. Pennington. Publisher: CPR Official)

The earlier years of the company were blighted by a number of losses which weakened an already struggling Gulf service to the benefit of the Canadian route which by 1880 had become the main source of income. At this time the Irish call was made at Queenstown but in the summer of 1886 it was transferred to either Belfast or Londonderry.

The smaller ships of the fleet invariably received names that ended with the suffix 'man', for example *Scotsman,* while the larger mail steamers took place names or those linked with imperialism, for example *Montreal* or *Dominion.* Occasionally, the Dominion Line used Bristol (Avonmouth) as its U.K. terminal and in 1896 started a new service between Liverpool and Boston, Massachusetts.

Although it never possessed large numbers of ships (in its fifty-six years of life it only ever owned forty-five ships), the Dominion Line provided a reliable and comfortable way of travel to Canada. So it was inevitable that, when John Pierpoint Morgan formed his monopoly-seeking International Mercantile Marine Company, the Dominion Line was a prime target for take-over bids. Morgan successfully took over Dominion Line and almost at the same time acquired the shares of the Leyland, American, Atlantic Transport, Red Star and, most importantly, the giant White Star Line of Liverpool.

The Morgan Group take-over occurred in February 1902 and immediately it began a process it dubbed its 'Steamship Amalgamation Plan'. This was, in reality, a device to ensure that the group's flagship company White Star got all the best routes and equipment. Hence in 1903, after only two round voyages for Dominion, the line lost its best ship, the new *Columbus,* to become White Star's *Republic* (see No. 76). The line's operations to Canada continued and in 1908 it ordered two large new liners, the *Albany* and *Alberta,* which were launched in September and December of that year. But, by the time the new vessels went down the slipway, they had been transferred to

94

129. **Empress of Scotland (1)** *(24,581 tons, Canadian Pacific). Launched as the largest ship in the world in 1905 by the Empress of Germany as* Kaiserin Auguste Victoria.
(Artist: Oswald F. Pennington. Publisher: CPR Official)

130. **Empress of Canada (1)** *(21,517 tons, Canadian Pacific). Built for the Company's transpacific service, this ship was lost serving as a troopship in 1943.* *(CPR Official)*

131. **Empress of England** *(25,585 tons, Canadian Pacific). Dating from 1956, this was the penultimate CP Empress. Today she is based in Miami as* Mardi Gras.
(Artist: John Smith. Publisher: Canadian Pacific)

White Star ownership and re-named *Megantic* and *Laurentic* (Nos. 138 to 140).

At the same time it was announced that the St. Lawrence services would be known as White Star-Dominion Line. The ostensible reason for the change, and it has some substance, was the emergence of the Canadian Pacific Railway's Steamship Company on the North Atlantic and the commissioning of its new *Empress of Britain* and *Empress of Ireland* (see No. 125). Whatever the reason, the *Laurentic* (Nos. 138 and 139), the first of two White Star ships to hold the name, got away on her maiden voyage from Liverpool on 29 April 1909 and the general travelling public soon recognised her as one of the most attractive ships that the line ever possessed. In 1911 she set a new record for the run, making the round voyage in thirteen days four hours. The *Megantic* (No. 140) also proved a useful addition to the fleet, but on the outbreak of war in 1914 the Canadian routes were severely restricted and both sisters became troop transports.

The *Laurentic* did not survive the conflict. Her loss led to one of the most outstanding salvage exploits in the history of deep sea diving. On 24 January 1917, while outward bound from Liverpool to Halifax, the *Laurentic* struck two mines that had been earlier laid off Malin Head, on the Northern Irish coast, by the German submarine U-80. The ship rapidly capsized and sank in 120ft. (37m) of water, taking with her 354 of the 475 people on board. In human terms it was the worst White Star tragedy of the war but *Laurentic* was carrying a cargo of 3,211 bars of gold bullion valued at £5 million. When the war ended, a team of Royal Navy divers under Commander G.C. Damant, R.N., set to work to recover the gold and succeeded by 1924 in recovering all but twenty-five of the bars, for a total investment on the part of the Treasury of £128,000!

The *Megantic* survived the war and made her first peace-time sailing of New York, so short was White Star of big liners for the mail

R.M.S. EMPRESS OF SCOTLAND, C.P.R. LINE
26,300 GROSS TONS   LENGTH 666 FT   BEAM 84 FT   SPEED 21 KNOTS

132. **Empress of Scotland (2)** *(26,032 tons, Canadian Pacific). The big transpacific service flier whose name was changed from* Empress of Japan *in 1942 when Japan came into the war.*
(Artist: John Nicholson. Publisher: Salmon)

service. Then she returned to Canadian routes but in 1920 she was switched to the London-Sydney service and even made a sailing to China in 1927 as a troopship. She finished her working life back on the North Atlantic and was broken up in 1933.

The name of the old Dominion Line was retained in the 1920s when the White Star Line launched two 16,000-ton liners, *Pittsburgh* (see No. 91) and *Regina* (Nos. 92 and 141), the latter ship spending her first two years, 1923-25, actually painted in Dominion Line colours, as illustrated in No. 141. Both ships were transferred to the Red Star Line, one in 1926 and the other in 1929. The Canadian service of White Star was thereafter maintained by the second *Laurentic* (see No. 85) until the merger with Cunard led to her withdrawal in 1936. So passed the White Star Line's Canadian services.

As we have seen in Chapter 3, the 150-year history of the Cunard Line had its origins in Canada and Halifax, Nova Scotia, was among

the first of the line's North American destinations. From there passengers went overland and by ferry feeder services to Quebec and Montreal. But it was not until 1911, when the Canadian Pacific, Allan, White Star and Canadian Northern lines were all well established, that Cunard made its first sailings down the St. Lawrence from the U.K.

The choice of home port for the service was Southampton and it was the shape of things to come. White Star had already moved to the Hampshire port in 1907 for its New York service, and, following the successful use of its facilities by the line's Canadian service ships, the New York Blue Riband service moved there in 1919. Cunard's Canadian services were to last until 1966, with Liverpool and Glasgow as alternative home ports to Southampton and the ships used fall into three groups, i.e. those constructed before, between and after the wars.

In May 1911, Cunard sailed three liners from U.K. ports to Quebec and Montreal within three weeks of each other. Two left from

133. **Royal Edward** *(11,117 tons, Canadian Northern) and her sister* Royal George *operated from Avonmouth to Canada from 1910 to 1914.* *(Artist: Odin Rosenvinge. Publisher: Barton)*

134. **Royal George's** *music room illustrated in an advertising card. The service claimed to be 'the fastest to Canada'.* *(Barton, Bristol)*

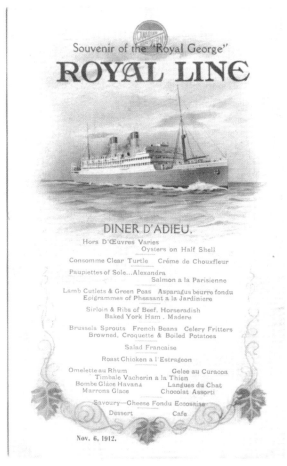

135. **Royal George's** *farewell dinner menu for 6 November 1912.*
It was issued as a postcard. (Barton, Bristol)

Southampton and the other from London and, although they differed in detail, they all possessed 'A' names and were all between 7,000 to 9,000 tons gross. *Ascania* (No. 142), *Ausonia* and *Albania* were later to be joined in 1913 by the larger *Alaunia* (13,405 tons gross) her sisters *Andania* and *Aurania* although the latter was not available until 1917 because of delays in building due to the priorities of war work.

The services introduced so thoroughly in

1911 proved a sound business venture and although the ageing *Albania* was sold in 1912, the remainder were brand new ships. The *Ascania* (No. 142) was a trim twin-funnelled craft from the famous Swan Hunter yard at Wallsend-on-Tyne and *Ausonia* came from the same builders, although she was single funnelled. Then came 1914 and war. Incredibly, all the 'A' liners of the Canadian service were lost, and all within the space of nineteen months between 30 May 1916 and 4 February

ROYAL LINER LEAVING AVONMOUTH, BRISTOL

136. **Royal Edward** *(11,117 tons, Canadian National) was torpedoed in the Aegean Sea, 14 September 1915, when trooping in the Gallipoli campaign. 935 people perished.* *(Barton, Bristol)*

1918. *Ascania* was wrecked in Newfoundland, *Alaunia* was mined and the other four were all torpedoed by U-boats.

The war's end found Cunard desperately short of tonnage and the company placed orders for thirteen new ships as soon as resources became available. Among these were six new liners of 14,000 tons, which differed so little in detail as to be defined as a class – the new 'A' class. The first three ships all sailed on their maiden voyages in June 1922, two from Southampton and the other from Liverpool. They were named *Andania* (Nos. 18 and 48), *Antonia* and *Ausonia* and they were followed in 1924/25 by *Aurania* (Nos. 49 and 63), *Alaunia* (No. 51) and finally *Ascania* (No. 50). All six quickly settled down on the Canadian run and demonstrated the advantages of an homogenous class of ship on a suitable route. They served without serious incident and profitably until 1939, when, on the outbreak of war, all six were requisitioned as armed merchant cruisers.

The second round with Germany was to prove equally expensive to Cunard in terms of loss of tonnage. The loss of life was less dramatic than in 1914-18 and only *Andania* was lost to enemy action, when she was torpedoed off Iceland on 15 June 1940 by a U-boat. She sank slowly and there appears to have been no loss of life. *Ascania* survived the war to return to Cunard service and re-opened the Quebec run in April 1949. The remaining four sisters were all bought by the Royal Navy for use as repair ships. This was probably a good financial deal for Sir Percy Bates, the Cunard chairman, as all the 'A' class were by then approaching twenty years of use, but it meant that in the first years of peace *Samaria* (Nos. 43 and 61) and *Scythia* (Nos. 44, 45 and 60) had to be transferred to the St. Lawrence and the Boston service dropped from the company's itinerary.

By 1953 the Cunard board were giving consideration to the replacement of four pre-war liners that maintained the Canadian service

Manchester Liners, Ltd., Oil Burning Turbine, S.S. "Manchester Regiment," 11,572 tons.
Manchester to Canada: 7½ days.

137. **Manchester Regiment** *(11,572 tons, Manchester Liners). One of the cargo liners with retractable funnel to navigate the Manchester Ship Canal, she carried passengers to Canada.*
(Artist: Walter Thomas. Publisher: James Haworth & Bros)

– *Franconia* (Nos. 53 to 55), *Samaria, Scythia* and *Ascania*. Four new liners were built between 1954 and 1957 and they were all given names that had been carried by earlier members of the Cunard fleet. The resultant ships were attractive 20,000 ton, single funnel, 19.5 knot vessels and all four came from the Clydebank yard of John Brown. The first ship *Saxonia* sailed on her maiden voyage from Liverpool on 2 September 1954 and *Ivernia, Carinthia* (No. 143) and *Sylvania* followed at approximately yearly intervals thereafter. They were the largest ships ever built by Cunard for the Canadian service and were ideal for the trade as long as it lasted. But airline competition had captured all the passenger bookings across the Atlantic by the early '60s and the Cunard Canadian services were withdrawn in 1966. The two ships on the run, *Carinthia* and *Sylvania*, were laid up and then sold to the Italian Sitmar Line for use on the Australian run, but they were both moored idle for two years in Southampton until taken to Italy for

rebuilding. They became *Fairland* and *Fairwind* under Italian ownership and eventually became part of P&O when that company bought Sitmar in 1989. Their sisters, *Saxonia* and *Ivernia* were refitted in 1962 and renamed *Carmania* (No. 70) and *Franconia* (Nos. 53 to 55). They were painted in green like *Caronia* and placed on full-time cruising. But being turbine driven steamships, they became ever more uncompetitive compared to motorships and in 1971 both were sold to the Soviet Union and renamed *Leonid Sobinov* and *Fedor Chaliapin*. The Russians used them for cruising with the objective of earning hard currency. Both were still in service in 1989.

By 1965, the number of passengers arriving in Canada by sea was down to 26,000 while the airlines carried 351,000. The writing was on the wall, but Canadian Pacific carried on the service until 23 November 1971 when *Empress of Canada* docked at Liverpool for the last time and ended sixty-eight years of service on the run to Canada.

138. **Laurentic** *(14,892 tons, White Star) went down in January 1917 with £5 million in gold bullion aboard. Most was recovered from 120 ft. of water by 1924.*

(Artist: Charles Dixon. Publisher: White Star)

139. **Laurentic** *at sea.*   *(Artist: Sam J.M. Brown. Publisher: Tuck OILETTE No. 9503)*

140. **Megantic** *(14,878 tons, White Star). This card is No. 139 reverse printed.*
(Artist: Sam J.M. Brown. Publisher: Tuck OILETTE No. 9503)

141. **Regina** *(16,314 tons, White Star) at Quebec. She served on this route from Liverpool until her sale*
to Red Star in 1929. *(Artist: Montague B. Black. Publisher: White Star)*

142. **Ascania (1)** *(9,111 tons, Cunard). An intermediate liner wrecked on the Newfoundland coast in 1918. The artist, Oliver, much exaggerates her size.*
(Artist: Richard Oliver. Publisher: Turner & Dunnett)

143. **Carinthia (3)** *(21,947 tons, Cunard), in a fine study by Charles Turner, seen in the St. Lawrence River, Quebec. Now in the P&O fleet.* *(Artist: C.E. Turner. Publisher: Thomas Forman)*

CHAPTER 5

The South Atlantic

Because the great spaces of the Atlantic Ocean saw the rise of the passenger liner to what has been described as its Golden Age and then witnessed its long decline, it is understandable that a large part of this book should be devoted to the history of ships that travelled on the North Atlantic routes. But other great journeys were made from European ports, often equalling the northern seas for danger and the need for stout physical courage. Before the coming of the steamship and planned schedules, sailing vessels left port only when a full load of passengers had been obtained for the trip. Then the traveller might find himself committed to anything up to six months' confinement in a small ship, on indifferent food, while the vessel might very well be rolling along in the gales of the Roaring Forties, or stuck becalmed in the heat of the tropics.

Any of these conditions could be met and have to be endured on the sea-lanes that ran south across the Equator to the Cape of Good Hope and the British colonies in South Africa, across the broad Atlantic and down to the emerging markets of South America. Many shipping companies arose and declined on these routes as the years went by but of those that managed to survive into the 1970s the two major lines were both British owned. These were the Union Castle Line which ran to South and East Africa, with calls at the Atlantic islands on the way, and the Royal Mail Steam Packet Company which serviced routes to Central South America.

The Union Castle Mail Steamship Company was formed in February 1900 by the merger of the two largest companies trading to the British colonies in South Africa. The Union Line dated from 1853 and its great rival, the Castle Line, had been founded by Sir Donald Currie in 1872. The Union Line was, in reality, the

brainchild of Arthur Anderson, one of the joint founders of P&O, and he created it as a fleet of colliers, designed to bring coal from South Wales to supply the steamer fleets using Southampton.

In 1854 the Crimean War broke out and the company's entire fleet was chartered by the British Government to carry supplies to the armies fighting in the far-off Crimean peninsula. This experience convinced the Union directors that their fleet was capable of far more than a coastal coal service and in 1856 they started a Southampton to Rio de Janeiro service, taking on the great Royal Mail Line in its own backyard.

The task proved too much for the Union Line and it was facing closure within a year. Then rescue appeared in the shape of a government contract to operate a monthly mail service to the Cape and Natal. The contract was for five years at £33,000 per annum. The Union Line's bid was accepted and the contract was the basis of its future success. In addition to the mail, the ships carried freight and passengers south and returned with wool, wine, brandy and large quantities of ostrich feathers for the fashion trade.

Conditions for passengers were primitive by today's standards but considered acceptable by contemporary travellers. Union were the first to provide bedding on African routes and also provided a stewardess. All lighting was by candles and these were put out promptly at 10 pm. There were no bathrooms and gentlemen made use of saltwater tubs available forward from 5 am to 7 am!

The Union vessels were usually given national names such as *Briton, Celt, Saxon* and *Dane.* As business developed, feeder services from Cape Town were started to smaller ports in both easterly and westerly directions. To

105

THE UNION CASTLE LINE ROYAL MAIL STEAMER "SAXON" (12385 tons)

144. **Saxon** *(12,385 tons, Union Castle). The last liner ordered for Union Line, she was transferred to Union Castle in the fitting out stage. Card used postally on 13 August 1906.* *(Union Castle)*

UNION-CASTLE LINE ROYAL MAIL STEAMER "KINFAUNS CASTLE." 9,656 TONS.

145. **Kinfauns Castle (2)** *(9,664 tons, Union Castle) served as an auxiliary cruiser in World War One, capturing two German vessels.* *(Union Castle)*

146. **Walmer Castle (2)** *(12,546 tons, Union Castle) was laid down as* Celt *for the Union Line but renamed when the lines merged. She served until 1932.* *(Union Castle)*

read the history of the line is to absorb a potted history of South Africa. As an example, during the Zulu War of 1879, Union ships were used to rush reinforcements to Natal after the victory of the Zulus at Isandalwana. The following year the *German* carried the Empress Eugénie to Durban from where she made a visit to the site in Zululand where her son Louis, the Prince Imperial, had been killed in action with the Zulus.

The Union was now well established but it always had to face keen competition from Donald Currie's Castle Line. Currie was born in Scotland in 1825 but was brought up in a large family in Belfast. In 1842 he moved to Liverpool where he joined Cunard as a freight clerk. Currie always cherished an ambition to own his own shipping business and in 1862 he managed to gain an interest in a small company trading across the North Sea from Scotland to Hamburg. He purchased four sailing vessels and went into business on the London-Cape Town-Calcutta route. Currie's Calcutta *Castles* (all his ships were named after castles) pros-

pered from the first. In 1865 he moved his headquarters from Liverpool to London and in 1871 ordered his first two *Castle* steamers, the *Dover Castle* and the *Walmer Castle*, which became the first *Castle* steamer to the Cape.

Thereafter Currie decided to concentrate on African trade, although his sailing ships still made the trip to Calcutta and the long voyage home via Cape Horn. Currie became an MP in 1880 and was knighted by Queen Victoria in 1881. The seeds of the eventual merger between the Union and Castle lines were sown as early as 1876 when the Cape Government awarded a joint mail contract to both companies. Although the terms of the contract specifically forbade the contractors to amalgamate and they were bitter and often acrimonious rivals, they now had to co-operate on the provision of the mail runs. Everything went well until the renewal of the mail contract was due again in 1900.

The Cape Government announced that only one company would get the contract, in an attempt to lower the price. Neither tendered

147. **Grantully Castle (2)** *(7,612 tons, Union Castle) was the last vessel to be built under Donald Currie who died on 13 April 1909.* *(Artist: William McDowell. Publisher: Union Castle)*

and the impasse was only resolved by the alliance of the two lines on 8 March 1990, when the Union Castle Mail Steamship Company Limited was registered. Sir Donald Currie became chairman and managing director, while the chairman of Union Line, Sir Francis Evans, and his directors joined the new board.

The colours of the Union Castle ships were distinctive. The hull was painted lavender grey with white upper works and the funnels were pale crimson with black tops. All the ships of the merged line received Castle names, except the mail steamers, such as the famous *Scot*, which carried on with their Union titles. Among the vessels that joined the Union Castle fleet at the merger was the last liner to be ordered for the Union Line. She was called *Saxon* (No. 144) and transferred to the Union Castle while in fitting out stage. She retained her name and sailed on for the new line until she was broken up in 1935.

The early years of this century saw the

Union Castle Line produce some very attractive liners for its South African routes and among these was the *Kinfauns Castle* (No. 145) which entered the mail service in 1899 and the larger *Walmer Castle* which had been ordered for the Union Line with the name *Celt* but which had been given a *Castle* name when the lines merged (No. 146).

The Union Castle line was unique in that it was the only big shipping company that did not lose a single major ship in the First World War. Following that war, larger ships were built and a round Africa service started in 1922. For these so-called intermediate services, Union Castle built considerable numbers of ships which carried cargo and passengers and offered trips to Africa at economic prices, providing the passenger did not have a strict schedule to maintain. A typical company intermediate ship was *Grantully Castle* of 1911 (No. 147). This ship and her sister *Garth Castle* were the last built for the line under the personal supervision of Sir Donald Currie who died on 13 April

THE UNION-CASTLE LINE ROYAL MAIL STEAMER "ARUNDEL CASTLE" (19,118 TONS)

148. **Arundel Castle (4)** *(19,118 tons, Union Castle) as she appeared after a major refit in 1937. Before that she sported four funnels.* *(Artist: William McDowell. Publisher: Union Castle)*

1909 at the age of eighty-three.

The first big liners to be built for the line after the First World War were the *Windsor Castle* and the *Arundel Castle* (No. 148). As built, these big 19,000-ton ships appeared with four funnels and were the largest ships built for the company to date. The *Arundel Castle* was the first to appear, sailing on her maiden voyage to Cape Town in April 1929. The *Windsor Castle* came out the following year and her naming caused some problems because a River Severn pleasure steamer already carried the name. This little ship had to be bought, renamed and then resold in order to free the name for use by the new liner. In 1937 both ships were modernised, given only two funnels and a rakish bow, looking much more attractive as seen in No. 148.

In the meanwhile, the Union Castle introduced the first in a long series of large motor vessels. This was the *Carnarvon Castle* of 1926 and the company used diesel engines for all their ships up to the Second World War.

Typical of a pre-war intermediate liner was the *Dunbar Castle* of 1930 (No. 149) and this series of motor ships culminated with the very attractive *Capetown Castle* of 1938 (No. 150).

The Union Castle Line was not so fortunate in the Second World War. When that war broke out, the company possessed thirty ships, All of them were relatively new, the average age of the fleet being ten years. Ten Union Castle ships were lost in action during the war and when it ended it was recorded that 274 crew lives had been lost while 144 bravery decorations had been won, as well as fifty-nine mentions in dispatches.

After the war new tonnage was ordered but in 1954 Union Castle was taken over by the British and Commonwealth Shipping Company, the London-based owners of the Clan Line. The new owners produced the largest vessels ever to sail on routes to Southern Africa. The new *Windsor Castle* of 1960 was a 37,000 ton monster, reflecting the development of South Africa's economy.

149. **Dunbar Castle (2)** *(10,002 tons, Union Castle) was mined in the English Channel in 1940, but her upper works remained above the water for six years.*

(Artist: William McDowell. Publisher: Union Castle)

Regular services were maintained throughout the '60s and early '70s, although the round Africa run was dropped in 1961. Then, as elsewhere in the world, passenger figures went into sharp decline and Union Castle announced that its final passenger sailing would take place on 12 August 1977, when the *Windsor Castle* left Southampton on her last voyage to the Cape. So closed over a century of tradition and of service to Africa.

Often seen sailing alongside Union Castle liners down the west coast of Africa were the black and buff funnels of the Elder Dempster Line of Liverpool. This company was formed in 1869 and was always recognised as the premier company trading to West Africa, particularly the Gold Coast and Nigeria. Much of the development of those countries was tied up with the fortunes of Elder Dempster. Apart from a large fleet of freighters, the company operated a passenger service from Liverpool, and later one from Southampton to West African ports.

Typical of its liners was the *Adda* (No. 165) which sailed on its maiden voyage in 1922. While carrying many tons of cargo, the ship had accommodation for 300 passengers which was a useful total when sailing on these routes. The Elder Dempster Company continued to offer passenger sailings up until 1974 when it gave in to airline competition and sold its flagship *Aureol* to Greek owners for further trading.

German companies were also prominent in the African trade and the German East Africa Line of Hamburg provided many services to and from West Africa, South Africa and on round the Cape to East Africa. A round Africa service was provided using the Suez Canal to return to Hamburg.

The Deutsche Ost Afrika was formed in 1890 by Adolf Woermann after the acquisition of German colonies in today's Tanzania. He also ran a company under his own name and, as the ships of both lines ran in the same colours, the two concerns appeared to be the same business.

150. **Capetown Castle** *(27,000 tons, Union Castle) was typical of the Union Castle motorships around the World War Two period.* *(Artist: William McDowell. Publisher: Union Castle)*

151. **Wadai** *(4,700 tons, Woermann) operated on the West African service, carrying 250 passengers. Seen here at Fernando Port.* *(Murmeister & Johler)*

152. **Adolf Woermann** *(6,000 tons, Woermann). Seen with another of the line's ships in Hamburg. The card was posted in Port Said, December 1928.* *(Hartung, Hamburg)*

At the outbreak of war in 1914, this company owned twenty-two steamers and typical of them was the *Adolf Woermann* (No. 152). This ship survived the war and sailed on until the 1930s. After the war, this company continued in the trade and provided small, efficient vessels like the *Wadai* (No. 151) of 1921 which is a good example of their equipment. In the 1920s they produced two further passenger ships, the *Ubena* and the *Watussi*. The final ships were the large liners *Pretoria* and *Windhuk*, 16,000 tons gross of 1936, both of which ended the Second World War as prizes of the victorious allies. The services did not resume after the war.

We have seen earlier in this chapter that it was the dominance of the Royal Mail Steam Packet Company that drove the Union Line off the Rio de Janeiro service in 1857 and Royal Mail were always the most prominent British concern to trade to the east coast of South America. To the Royal Mail must be added the names of Pacific Steam Navigation, the Nelson Line, Blue Star and Booth of Liverpool.

The Royal Mail Steam Packet Company was founded as long ago as July 1839 and incorporated by royal charter the same year. The charter clearly defined the objects of the business as 'the conveyance of the mails to and from … South America and for this purpose to establish a regular supply of steam and other vessels'.

The first decade of its history saw Royal Mail almost exclusively engaged in the mail run to the West Indies but in 1850 it started the run down to Rio, Montevideo and Buenos Aires for which it became famous and on which it prospered. Most of its early ships were given the names of rivers, but later ethnic names of Spanish and South American origin were added. Southampton was the home terminal but London was added in 1880 and by 1895 the line owned twenty-seven ships, although in these years its fortunes were always fluctuating.

Typical of the ships being operated at this

THE PACIFIC STEAM NAVIGATION COMPANY

Triple-Screw R.M.S. "ORDUÑA," 25,230 Tons Displacement.

153. **Orduna** *(15,507 tons, Pacific Steam) and her sister* Orbita *sailed around Cape Horn to Valparaiso in her early career.* *(Andrew Reid & Co.)*

time was the *Danube* of 1893 (No. 155) a 6,000 ton ship that could steam at fifteen knots. *Danube's* accommodation was considered sufficiently good for her to host the members of the House of Lords who attended the naval review at Spithead to celebrate Queen Victoria's Diamond Jubilee in 1897.

A significant event in 1903 was the appointment of Owen Philipps (later Lord Kylsant) as Chairman of Royal Mail in March of that year. Philipps was the prototype of the twentieth century commercial tycoon and his prime objective was to make Royal Mail the monopoly force in British shipping. In this he almost succeeded and over the next twenty-five years he bought out company after company including White Star at the end of 1926.

Among the many ships of the Kylsant years were the 'A' ships of 1906-8. They set a fashion for the line of graceful one-funnel ships of which *Asturias* of 1908 was typical. In 1923, she was renamed *Arcadian* and was employed full-time cruising, a trade in which Royal Mail

were early specialists (No. 156). An improved version of *Asturias* was the *Andes* of 1913 and she was one of a class of four. While serving as an auxiliary cruiser in 1917 with her sister ship *Alcantara, Andes* was in a gun duel with the German raider *Greif* which resulted in the destruction of both *Greif* and *Alcantara*. In 1929 *Andes* was painted white, renamed *Atlantis* and sent cruising (No. 157). In this role she became very well known, and more so in the 1939 war for her service as a hospital ship engaged in the repatriation of prisoners-of-war. She was scrapped in 1952.

Royal Mail lost fifteen ships in the First World War and much second-hand tonnage was bought in to replace the losses. Philipps was made a Baron, as Lord Kylsant, in 1923 and continued his expansion plans. By 1929 he had overreached the company's financial resources which eventually forced his group into liquidation and himself into prison, sentenced for financial offences committed in a forlorn attempt to save the company. A new company

154. **Reina del Pacifico** *(17,702 tons, Pacific Steam) entered the South American trade in 1931. She did an annual cruise round the South American continent.*
(Artist: James S. Mann. Publisher: Andrew Reid & Co.)

Royal Mail Lines Limited was registered in 1932. Lord Essendon was the first Chairman.

Among the ships taken over by the new concern were two 22,000 ton motor ships, *Alcantara* (No. 161) and *Asturias* ordered from Harland and Wolff in 1924 and delivered in 1926 and 1927. The engines gave a speed of sixteen knots and when the first ship *Asturias* came out she was the largest motor ship in existence. Both ships had good accommodation but their service speed was slow and they vibrated badly. In 1934 they were returned to their builders for the fitting of steam turbines, lengthened funnels and a 10ft. (3m) extension to the bows. They emerged three knots faster and much better looking. Both served as auxiliary cruisers in the Second World War and in July 1940 *Alcantara* fought a bruising action with the German raider *Thor*. After the war, they both lost their forward funnel which was a dummy and had been removed for war service. They were broken up in 1958.

Following the 1932 crash of the Kylsant group, Royal Mail absorbed the ships of the

Nelson Line which had been purchased originally in 1913 but allowed to run independently. The Nelson company had been founded by a firm of Liverpool butchers to import beef from the Argentine and in 1910 had started to carry passengers. The Nelson ships wore distinctive colours and were generally around 7,000 tons, taking twenty-one days between London and Buenos Aires (No. 160).

In 1927 the line ordered five new ships twice the size of anything previously owned. All Nelson ships had the prefix 'Highland' to their name and *Highland Monarch* was the first to be completed. She sailed for the River Plate on 18 October 1928 and was followed by *Highland Brigade, Highland Chieftain, Highland Patriot, Highland Princess* (No. 158) and *Highland Hope*, the last running aground on the Portuguese coast in 1930. In Nelson colours the ships looked very splendid (No. 159) but in 1932 they were all absorbed into the Royal Mail fleet.

Another company associated closely with Royal Mail was the Pacific Steam Navigation

155. **Danube** (5,891 tons, Royal Mail) was used as host ship for the House of Lords at the Royal Naval Review at Spithead in 1897. (Artist: Neville Cunning. Publisher: Tuck OILETTE No. 9151)

which dated from 1838. It passed into Royal Mail ownership in 1910, becoming independent again in 1932. Among many attractive ships that sailed on PSN services to the west coast of South America were *Orbita* and *Orduna* of 1914 (No. 153) and the 17,000 ton *Reina del Pacifico*, a motor ship built in 1931 (No. 154).

The next liner for Royal Mail, and their last operational passenger ship, was the *Andes*, 27,000 tons, built in 1939 (No. 166). She was the largest ship ever built for the company, but her maiden trip to the River Plate was interrupted by seven years acting as a valuable troopship in the Second World War. In 1960 she was put on permanent cruising and her withdrawal in 1971 meant the end of Royal Mail passenger operations.

Three other British lines deserve mention for their operations to South America. The Blue Star Line was founded by the Vestey family in 1911 to operate in the frozen meat trade from the Argentine. From 1929 to 1969 they carried passengers and started the service with five

13,000 ton ships of which *Avila* (No. 162) was one. Later she became *Avila Star* and was lost in the war in July 1942.

The Booth Line of Liverpool, which named all its ships after early Christian saints, offered a passenger service up the Amazon to Manaos from 1866 to 1964. The *Anselm* of 1905 (No. 163) was the second of four ships to carry the name. The Booth Line became part of the Vestey group in 1946, preceded by Lamport and Holt two years earlier.

Lamport and Holt first operated services to South America in 1866 and in their day were big in passenger services, which they also operated from New York. Their last two passenger ships were *Vandyck* and *Voltaire* (No. 164) which spent from 1932 onwards in a very successful cruising programme. They were both lost during World War Two.

Since 1969, when Royal Mail withdrew, it has only been possible to get to South America from Europe by the odd freighter or in an aircraft, spelling the end of a great sea service tradition.

R.M.S.P. "ARCADIAN" IN NORWEGIAN FJORDS—DAWN.

156. **Arcadian** *(12,015 tons, Royal Mail). Launched as* Asturias *in 1908, she was renamed* Arcadian *and refitted for full-time cruising in 1923.* *(Artist: Kenneth Shoesmith. Publisher: Royal Mail)*

ROYAL MAIL LINE CRUISING VESSEL "ATLANTIS" AT MADEIRA

157. **Atlantis** *(15,620 tons, Royal Mail) was the most famous British cruise ship of the 1930s. She began her career as* Andes *in 1913.* *(Artist: Kenneth Shoesmith. Publisher: Royal Mail)*

ROYAL MAIL MOTOR VESSELS — 14,500 TONS GROSS — SOUTH AMERICAN SERVICE
'HIGHLAND BRIGADE' 'HIGHLAND CHIEFTAIN' 'HIGHLAND MONARCH' 'HIGHLAND PRINCESS'

158. **Highland Princess** *(14,620 tons, Royal Mail). Fifty-two years after her launch in 1930, this ex-Nelson Line motor vessel was still in service as the Chinese* Guang Ha. *(Artist: Kenneth Shoesmith. Publisher: Royal Mail)*

A NELSON LINER.

FAST MAIL PASSENGER AND FREIGHT SERVICES TO SPAIN, PORTUGAL, CANARY ISLANDS, BRAZIL, URUGUAY, AND ARGENTINE

159. *Highland Class motor vessel in Nelson Line colours.* (Artist: Odin Rosenvinge)

160. **Highland Rover** *(7,244 tons, Nelson Line). First of a new class of passenger liners, she took twenty-one days between London and Buenos Aires.* *(H&J Ltd)*

161. **Alcantara** *(22,607 tons, Royal Mail). Launched in 1926 as the largest motor vessel in the world, she was converted to steam turbines in 1934. This view shows her post-war.* *(Royal Mail)*

Luxurious Comfort—No Emigrants or Second-class.

162. **Avila Star** *(12,872 tons, Blue Star). One of a class of five ordered in 1925,* Avila Star *was torpedoed and sunk by U-201 near the Azores in July 1942.* (Artist: Ellis Silas. Publisher: Blue Star)

BOOTH LINE.   R.M.S. ANSELM.

163. **Anselm** *(5,442 tons, Booth Line) served on the River Amazon service to Manaos. She collided with and sank her sister vessel* Cyril *in the Amazon in September 1905.*
(Artist: Norman Wilkinson. Publisher: Booth Official)

164. **Voltaire** *(13,248 tons, Lamport & Holt). She and her sister* Vandyck were *well known as cruising ships in the 1930s.* Voltaire *was sunk by the German raider* Thor *in 1941.*
(Artist: Walter Thomas. Publisher: Liverpool P&S)

165. **Adda** *(7,800 tons, Elder Dempster) carried 300 passengers on the West Africa service.*
(Artist: Odin Rosenvinge. Publisher: Turner & Dunnett)

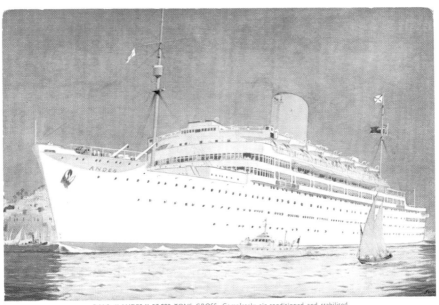

R.M.S. "ANDES" 27,000 TONS GROSS. Completely air-conditioned and stabilised.
Royal Mail Lines Sunshine Cruises to the Mediterranean, Northern Capitals, West Indies, etc.

166. **Andes** *(27,000 tons, Royal Mail). The large popular cruising liner of the 1960s.* *(Royal Mail)*

CHAPTER 6

India, the Indies, Australasia and the Far East

From the days that Marco Polo returned from his travels with tales of Tartary and the riches of the Orient, travel to the Far East has exercised an obsessive fascination for Europeans. Nowhere was this more so than in the United Kingdom from whose ports sailed at least two of the early circumnavigators, Drake and Woodes Rodgers, and from where the great James Cook first set out on his voyages to open up the Australian continent to European colonisation.

In the early days of trade to the east, the primary commodity sought by merchants from the west was spices but as the industrial revolution swept through Europe the demand for raw materials, such as wool from Australia, feeding stuffs, jute and cotton from India and all the tea that could be carried, led to the development of fast sailing ships which have gone into maritime history as 'clippers'.

With the introduction of the steam engine for use in ship propulsion during the third decade of the nineteenth century, the stage was set for the foundation of one of the greatest shipping companies ever and one that continues to hold a predominant position in today's commercial world. The origins of the great P&O go back as far as 1836 when two London merchants, Arthur Anderson and Brodie Wilcox, chartered their first steamer to trade to Spain as agents for the Peninsular Steam Navigation Company. In the following year the partners obtained an Admiralty contract to carry mails between Lisbon, Cadiz and Gibraltar.

Three years after that, in 1840, the line picked up another contract, this time to take the mails all the way to Alexandria, where they would go overland to Suez and be carried on to India by ships sailing down the Red Sea. A railway was built in due course between Port Said and Suez for the purpose. Accordingly, the

name of the firm was changed to Peninsular and Oriental Steam Navigation Company which was soon shortened to the colloquial P&O. By 1854, the line had taken over the Suez to Bombay route to India, and added services to Singapore, Hong Kong and Sydney.

The opening of the Suez Canal in 1870 produced an upheaval in P&O arrangements, and it coincided with the need to re-engine many of its ships with the new compound steam engines, which were more efficient than the simple expansion type fitted in most steamers up to that time. The changes were made, and by the late nineteenth century, P&O were regarded as the 'Cunard of the East' and almost a pillar of the British state. At this time the line reflected all the military dignity and conservatism of the British officers and civil servants who occupied its first-class quarters on leisurely voyages to and from the Far East. Its ships were never fast or large, but they were well suited to the trade and were always in receipt of government support in the shape of mail or trooping contracts. Before the First World War, few P&O ships could make more than twelve knots and even their colours were restrained – black hulls with stone upper works and black funnels.

P&O were never in the van of technical advance during those years of the nineteenth century, preferring to retain reciprocating engines for all its ships until the late 1920s. However, it did produce twin-screw vessels, not because of speed requirements but to avoid the embarrassment of a broken shaft in eastern seas, far away from the skills of a European shipyard.

The liner *Himalaya* (No. 167) of 1894 was the first modern vessel in every sense of the term to serve on the eastern routes. Together with her sister *Australia,* she was capable of

167. **Himalaya** *(6,900 tons, P&O). Built in 1894 to double on either India or Australia routes, Himalaya introduced modern bathrooms to the eastern routes.* *(Andrew Reid & Co.)*

168. **Devanha** *(8,092 tons, P&O). One of four sisters built in 1903 for the India – China service.* *(Andrew Reid & Co.)*

123

P. & O. S.S. "CHINA" LEAVING MARSEILLES.
8,000 TONS, 11,000 HORSE-POWER

169. **China** *(7,900 tons, P&O) and four sisters were built in 1896 for the express service between Marseilles and Bombay via Suez.* *(Artist: Wm. L. Wyllie. Publisher: P&O)*

operating to India and Australia, and once carried the mails from Adelaide to London in twenty-six days sixteen hours. *Himalaya* was a popular ship on the Australian services for the reason that she introduced the modern style bathroom to the high seas and her accommodation was an appreciable advance over existing ships. The second ship of the fleet to carry the name, she had a long career and was an old ship when she was requisitioned in 1914 by the Admiralty to become an armed merchant cruiser. She was fitted out at Hong Kong with eight 4.7 inch guns and patrolled the China Sea as a commerce protection unit.

The *Himalaya* and the *Australia* were followed in 1894 by the *Caledonia,* a slightly larger but very similar ship. When she came out the *Caledonia* looked lovely in white hull and buff funnels, but two years later she reverted to the company's dowdy traditional colours. Thus she heralded the attractive livery that the company adopted for its larger passenger ships over thirty years later.

In the earlier years of this century, it was unusual for P&O to build a single ship of one design. More often a pair of vessels would emerge and frequently a whole class. This was particularly so with the intermediate ships that handled the secondary services away from the mail routes. Typical of this practice was the D-Class of 1903 – *Delhi, Delta, Dongola* and *Devanha* – built to operate on the India to China service. This class, of which *Devanha* (No. 168) is illustrated, were slightly over 8,000 tons and could achieve sixteen knots, proving both popular and profitable. *Devanha* was used as a troopship at the Gallipoli landings in 1915, carrying the Australian 12th Division. The troops were landed in the ship's boats, towed by destroyers, while the ship herself steamed closer inshore to divert the fire of the Turkish guns. The 12th Battalion suffered heavy casualties on the beaches. One of the *Devanha's* lifeboats was recovered from the operation and now rests, bullet torn, in the Australian War Museum at Canberra.

The *Himalaya* and her sisters were followed by another class of mail ships in 1896, all named after eastern countries. *India, China, Persia, Arabia* and *Egypt.* P&O vessels called

170. **Balranald** *(13,039 tons, P&O). One of five 'one-class' liners built in 1921 for the Australian service. All five had been scrapped by 1936.* *(Artist: Frank Mason. Publisher: P&O)*

at this time at Marseilles to collect passengers who had travelled overland from London via Dover-Calais and Paris. No. 169 shows *China* leaving that port on the first leg of the run to Port Said. These ships also had the advantage that they could carry 2,500 troops.

The *Egypt* (No. 172) was the last of the class to be completed and was thus the last P&O ship to be driven by a single screw. She was destined to take her place in the history of marine salvage when, in thick fog in the Bay of Biscay in 1922, the twenty-five year old liner was in collision and sank in seventy fathoms with the loss of ninety-six lives – twelve passengers and eighty-four crew. On board was bullion valued at a 1922 price of £1,054,000. So deep was the wreck and its true position unknown, due to the fog, that Lloyds, the London underwriters, paid in full. Nevertheless, over a period of seven Biscay seasons which ended in 1932, the Italian salvage company Sorima recovered the bullion, using several new techniques, including the first use of pressure chambers. The search for the *Egypt's* gold made headlines at the time but is now largely forgotten.

The next set of large mail steamers for the company was the 'M' class which were twin screw and started to appear from the shipyards in 1903. The *Mooltan* (No. 171) was nearly 10,000 tons gross and other ships of the class, such as *Mantua* of 1909 (No. 173), would top that figure. Most of these ships were introduced on to the Bombay route. Then, when they had settled down, they were transferred to either the Australian or Far East services.

The year 1914 was to prove memorable in the history of P&O and not only for the Great War which broke out on 4 August of that year. On 23 May, the City was astounded to hear that P&O were to merge with the British India Steam Navigation Company, a shipping giant that dated back to 1856. The new combine was to be headed by B&I's chairman, Lord Inchcape, who continued to head the joint enterprise until his death in 1932. On 28 June 1914, the Caird yard at Greenock launched the largest P&O ship to date, the 11,518 ton *Kaisar-I-Hind* (No. 174) which, despite the war, sailed on the maiden voyage to Bombay on 24 October.

P. & O. S.S. "MOOLTAN" AT MALTA.
10,000 TONS, 15,000 HORSE-POWER.

171.   **Mooltan**   (1)
*(9,500 tons, P&O) built
in 1903, pictured at St.
Angelo, Malta.
(Artist: Wm. L. Wyllie.
Publisher: P&O)*

At the start of the First World War, the joint P&O and B&I lines had two hundred ships at sea. Within three months over one hundred had been called up for war service, and by the war's end ninety-eight vessels had been lost to enemy action, including the *India* and the *Persia*. The latter had been lost to a U-boat off Crete with a loss of 335 lives.

But the war was not always a period of loss. Always convinced of the certainty of victory, Lord Inchcape maintained considerable plans for future expansion and in 1916 he took control of the New Zealand Shipping Company and it subsidiary, the Federal Steam Navigation

Company. This was a logical extension of the business but it says much for Inchcape's business acumen that he was prepared to take these decisions at the height of the worst war that the country had fought for generations. The companies concerned continued to trade under the same colours and organisation. A typical New Zealand Shipping Company liner of the period was the *Ruahine* of 1909 (No. 189), while the attractive characteristics of a Federal liner show up well in the illustration of *Dorset* (No. 188), which served on the Pacific routes to New Zealand.

A year later, the Union Steamship Company

172. **Egypt** *(7,912 tons, P&O) was the last single screw ship built for P&O. She was lost in a collision in the English Channel off Ushant in May 1922 with eighty-six deaths. She had £1.05 million in bullion on board.* *(Artist: J Simpson. Publisher: Tuck OILETTE No. 9112)*

P. & O. R.M.S. MANTUA, 11,000 TONS, 15,000 HORSE POWER.
India and China Mail and Passenger Service.

173. **Mantua** *(10,885 tons, P&O) was used mainly on the Far East route.*
(Artist: Frank Mason. Publisher: P&O)

P. & O. S.S. "KAISAR-I-HIND."
(11,518 TONS, 16,000 HORSE-POWER.)

174. **Kaisar-I-Hind** *(11,518 tons, P&O). A very popular ship between London and Bombay.*
(Artist: Charles Dixon. Publisher: P&O)

of New Zealand was added to the P&O empire together with several smaller companies which added 107 ships totalling 370,000 tons gross to the group, including their trade routes and goodwill.

Take-overs were a not infrequent occurrence in the history of P&O. One of the most well known was the purchase of Lund's Blue Anchor in 1910, after that company's flagship, the 9,000 ton *Waratah,* disappeared without trace in 1909 while homeward bound between Durban and Cape Town. No sign of the ship or the 211 people on board was ever found. The Blue Anchor Line specialised in carrying emigrants at the lowest possible rates via the Cape of Good Hope. The purchase allowed P&O to enter the trade for an investment of £275,000 and the ships became known as the P&O Branch Line. Among the vessels acquired was the *Narrung* (No. 185).

Other purchases in this second decade of the century were a controlling interest in the Orient Line (to which we shall return) and the take-over of the Khedivial Mail Line, an Egyptian

based operator which sailed in the Eastern Mediterranean and the Black Sea. This latter company proved to be a rarity in P&O history – a loss maker – and, because he felt personal responsibility for this, Lord Inchcape privately bought all the shares in 1924. The line eventually passed back to Alexandria owners. *Khedive Ismail,* built as *Aconcagua* by Scotts of Greenock in 1922 (No. 193), was typical of the line's ships when it was owned by the Pharaonic Company in the 1930s.

The end of the war saw an active period of rebuilding for P&O and one of the first orders was to resurrect a contract delayed by hostilities for five Branch liners to carry on the Blue Anchor services. Among these was *Balranald* of 1921 (No. 170) and she and her four sisters kept up the emigrant service until its withdrawal in 1936 when all five B-class liners were scrapped.

Among the largest post-war buildings was the *Mongolia* (No. 175) of 16,000 tons in 1923 and then the same year saw the first company ships to exceed 20,000 tons, the *Malohja* and

P. & O. INDIA-CHINA-AUSTRALIA
MAIL AND PASSENGER SERVICES.

S.S. "MONGOLIA" | 16,000 TONS.
13,000 H.P.

175. **Mongolia** *(16,385 tons, P&O) served P&O from 1923 to 1938 when she was chartered to the New Zealand Line and later sold in Panama.* *(Artist: Jack Spurling. Publisher: P&O)*

the *Mooltan* (No. 179). Both these famous ships survived the Second World War to last until 1954, but the following ships, the 'R' and 'C' classes ordered in 1925, were to suffer huge losses. Five of the seven ships that made up the two classes were lost to enemy action and these included *Rajputana* (No. 176) and *Comorin* (No. 177). Of the 'R' class, the most famous is the heroic *Rawalpindi* which, on patrol as an armed merchant cruiser in the North Sea on 23 November 1939, sighted the German battle cruisers *Scharnhorst* and *Gneisenau*. Heavily out-gunned, *Rawalpindi* accepted action but was soon a blazing wreck. She sank, taking Captain Kennedy and 269 crew with her. Captain Kennedy was the father of the author and television presenter Ludovic Kennedy.

By 1930, P&O had gone over to turbine machinery and their *Viceroy of India* (No. 178) of 1929 was the first large ship to have turbo-electric propulsion. Also a war loss, off North Africa in 1942, the *Viceroy,* as she was always known, is for many the most popular P&O liner. She was followed by a series of ships that

were modern, large express liners called the *Straths* and painted in the now familiar white hulls and buff funnels.

After the Second World War, in which it again suffered losses, P&O found itself in a very different world. Britain had quit India and the mail contracts had gone to the airlines. But much trade continued to exist in the east and a series of new ships appeared such as *Chusan,* yet another *Himalaya* and *Arcadia.* In 1960 the passenger services were merged with Orient Line vessels and 1961 saw the largest passenger liner to be built at Belfast since the *Titanic,* the much loved 45,000 ton *Canberra* which continued in service until 1977. Like many other large companies, P&O has diversified its interests to meet modern conditions and today, while still owning a large fleet of cruise liners based in America where the market continues to expand, it has building companies, ferry operations, container lines, road haulage and finance houses numbered among its interests, under the challenging leadership of Lord Stirling.

176. **Rajputana** *(16,568 tons, P&O), a sister of the heroic* Rawalpindi, *was sunk by UB-108 west of Ireland in April 1941.* *(Artist: Jack Spurling. Publisher: P&O)*

177. **Comorin** *(15,116 tons, P&O) was another P&O liner from the 1920s that was lost in World War Two.* *(Artist: Jack Spurling. Publisher: P&O)*

P. & O. S.S. Viceroy of India, 19,700 Tons Gross.
India Mail and Passenger Service.

178. **Viceroy of India**
(19,648 tons, P&O). A popular ship, she was unusual in her day for using turbo-electric propulsion.
(Artist: Jack Spurling. Publisher: P&O)

The Orient Line, the other great British company on the eastern routes, could trace its origins back to the Thompsons, a London firm of shipping agents and brokers who were active as early as 1820, although the line was not registered until 1878 as the Orient Steam Navigation Company. Its first ships were chartered tonnage from Pacific Steam who had over-estimated the South American market and had surplus capacity.

The venture was successful from the start, and although they were in direct competition with the great P&O, the Orient directors were so encouraged by the results that they soon ordered their first liner, the four-masted, 5,000 ton *Orient* of 1879. When she emerged, *Orient* was considered better than anything then owned by the rival company and she established a long tradition of popular Orient ships, all of which carried names beginning with the letter O. In 1888 the Orient won a share with P&O of the valuable Australian mail contract and, although it maintained links with Pacific Steam and later Royal Mail, this year saw the start of close collaboration with the larger company. Orient kept its grip on the mail contracts with such ships as *Orontes* of 1902 (No. 180). *Orontes* made fifty-three round

179. **Mooltan** *(20,847 tons, P&O). A spirited Spurling study which makes no concessions to 'queasy'*
would-be passengers. *(Artist: Jack Spurling. Publisher: P&O)*

voyages between London and Sydney in the period from her maiden voyage in October 1902 until the outbreak of war in 1914.

Orontes was followed by a splendid class of six 12,000 ton ships which date from 1909, and once again Orient had produced superior equipment to anything owned by P&O.

A member of this class was *Otranto* (No. 181) which became the best known Orient liner of the period though for reasons unconnected with her services to the line. In 1914 she was requisitioned and converted into an armed liner and sent to join Admiral Craddock's squadron in the South Atlantic. Craddock was under orders to search out the German East Asiatic Squadron which was attempting to return to Germany via Cape Horn. Craddock was one of the most popular officers in the navy and his opponent was the charismatic and chivalrous Admiral Graf von Spee. The clash between the two flotillas off the Chilean coast on 1 November 1914 was a complete German victory, Craddock losing his flagship and his life. A modern naval action is no place for

passenger liners and Craddock's last order before his bridge was shot from under him was for *Otranto* to escape. This she just succeeded in doing.

Later in the war *Otranto* made the headlines again and in an even more tragic manner. By 1918 she had become a troopship engaged in bringing the US Army to the battlefields of Europe. On 6 October 1918, while sailing in convoy off the Hebridean island of Islay, *Otranto* was rammed by the P&O *Kashmir* and completely disabled in storm force conditions. She ran aground on Islay and broke up, 370 lives being lost in the tragedy.

Another ship of this class, *Otway*, became a war loss, being torpedoed on 22 July 1917 by UC-49 while acting as a member of the famous 10th Cruiser Squadron. One of the sisters, *Orvieto* (No. 182), served for a period as a minelayer in the North Sea.

After the war, in which four ships had been lost, 51% of Orient shares were acquired in 1919 by P&O, although Orient kept its separate identity. The first ship to join the fleet was the

180. **Orontes** *(9,028 tons, Orient Line) made fifty-three round voyages London to Sydney from 1902 to 1914.* *(Artist: Charles Dixon. Publisher: Orient Official)*

181. **Otranto** *(12,124 tons, Orient Line) was at the Battle of Coronel in November 1914 as an auxiliary cruiser.* *(Artist: Charles Dixon. Publisher: Orient Official)*

133

182. **Orvieto** *(12,133 tons, Orient Line), a sister of* Otranto, *was used for mine-laying in World War One.*
(Artist: Charles Dixon. Publisher: Orient Official)

Ormonde (No. 183) which was followed by five 20,000 ton ships which formed the backbone of the line between the wars.

Heavy losses were suffered again in the Second World War with Germany, four of Orient's eight liners being lost and a big rebuilding programme was started. Three large liners were built, the first of which was the *Orcades* (No. 184) which sailed on her maiden voyage in 1948. The last Orient liner was the big *Oriana* of 1960; 41,923 tons gross, but by the time she was completed, the line had been fully merged with P&O.

Other prominent companies to provide services to the east over the years have been the Bibby, Blue Funnel, Anchor and Ellerman lines.

The Bibby Line of Liverpool first offered services from that port to India and Burma in 1891 and this became a fortnightly schedule from 1900 onwards. Bibby was noted for its 'house style' long before modern advertising hype and its graceful four-masted ships were well known. It was also a pioneer of the motor

ship and *Oxfordshire* of 1912 (No. 186) was the last steamship in the fleet. *Staffordshire* (No. 187) was typical of a number of inter-war Bibby ships which were named after English counties.

The name Blue Funnel Line was the trading title of Alfred Holt and Company of Liverpool, which was primarily a deep sea freight concern which carried a few first-class passengers to provide useful additional revenue. Legend has it that when Alfred Holt bought his first ship in 1852 he found some spare cans of blue paint on board and used it to paint the funnel, so starting a great tradition of the high seas. The line has prospered ever since and No. 190 shows one of the many Blue Star liners sailing off Gibraltar in a post-Second World War study by Walter Thomas.

From 1882 to 1966, the Anchor Line of Glasgow, in addition to its New York service, ran via the Suez Canal to Bombay. In fact, it was an Anchor ship, *Dido,* that made the first British passage of the Suez Canal in 1869. The company ran a series of small liners of which *Castalia* (No. 191) was typical.

183. **Ormonde** *(14,981 tons, Orient Line) was completed in 1917 and served until 1952, with a brilliant record of trooping in World War Two.* *(Artist: B. Gribble. Publisher: Tuck OILETTE)*

184. **Orcades** *(28,472 tons, Orient Line) was built to replace war losses.*
(Artist: John Nicholson. Publisher: Salmon)

135

185. **Narrung** *(5,800 tons, Lund's Blue Anchor Line). Used in the emigrant trade, these three ships were bought by P&O in 1910, following the loss of* Waratah. *(Blue Anchor Official)*

The famous name of Ellerman was prominent among British owners for most of this century. By 1939 it was a large conglomerate built up by the late Sir John Ellerman and controlling a dozen lines. Although it traded to the East, it was also large in East African trade and its ships, all city names, were seen world-wide. *City of Paris* (No. 192) dates from 1922 and could carry two hundred passengers. After fourteen years in the Indian trade, she was transferred to the London-Cape Town-Beira route in 1936.

No account of Far Eastern services would be complete without mention of the Japanese merchant service and, in particular, of the great Nippon Yusen Kabusiki Kaisya (NYK Line) which dates back to 1868. It established a European service in 1896 and offered world services up until 1939. Its ships were wiped out in the Pacific campaigns of 1941-45 and it never returned as a large operator of passenger ships. Three of its inter-war ships, *Suwa Maru* (No. 194), *Taiyo Maru* (No. 195) and *Haruna Maru* (No. 196) are illustrated.

Finally, the Greeks and, in particular, the Chandris family of Piraeus. The family have been shipowners since 1911 and owned a considerable fleet of tramp steamers before the Second World War. Their importance in the Australian passenger trade arises from their purchase of redundant liners in the late fifties for use in the then buoyant emigrant trade. Among these was the *Patris* (No. 198), an ex-Union Castle ship destined originally for African routes. She made her first voyage to Sydney for Chandris in December 1959 and was followed by several others including the old US Line's flagship *America*. Typical of Chandris operations was the purchase of the American liner *Monterey* (No. 199) which was built for the Matson Line's Hawaii service. After several name changes she became Chandris' *Britanis* (No. 200) in 1970 and was put on a round the world service – Southampton–Sydney–Southampton. The emigrant trade had all but vanished by 1975 and *Britanis* was transferred to full-time cruising.

186. **Oxfordshire** *(8,600 tons, Bibby) came from Harland and Wolff in 1912 and set a fashion for four-masted Bibby liners.* *(Artist: James S. Mann. Publisher: Bibby)*

187. **Staffordshire** *(10,654 ton, Bibby). Built for the Liverpool – Rangoon Service, she was completed in 1929 with Sulzer diesels.* *(Artist: James S. Mann. Publisher: Bibby)*

188. **Dorset** *(8,695 tons, Federal) served on the Pacific route to New Zealand.*
(Artist: Charles de Lacey. Publisher: Federal)

189. **Ruahine** *(10,758 tons, NZ Shipping Company) served NZ Shipping from 1909 until her sale to Italy in 1949.* *(Artist: Charles Dixon. Publisher: NZ Shipping Company)*

190. *Blue Funnel Line (name of vessel unknown) seen off Gibraltar, post-World War Two.*
(Artist: Walter Thomas. Publisher: Thomas Forman)

ANCHOR LINE S.S. "CASTALIA" (INDIA SERVICE).

191. **Castalia** *(6,715 tons, Anchor) was famous for beating off a U-boat attack in the Mediterranean in*
1916. *(Artist: Odin Rosenvinge. Publisher: Turner & Dunnett)*

ELLERMAN'S CITY LINE TO AND FROM INDIA, CEYLON, AND EGYPT.

192. **City of Paris** *(10,902, Ellerman) and* City of Nagpur *maintained Ellerman India services until 1936 when they were transferred to East Africa.*
(Artist: Odin Rosenvinge. Publisher: Turner & Dunnett)

193. **Khedive Ismail** *(12,000 tons, Pharaonic) was active in the Mediterranean in the late 1930s.*
(Artist: Frank Mason. Publisher: Thomas Forman)

194. **Suwa Maru** *(10,927 tons, NYK Line) operated between Europe and Japan. She was lost to a submarine in 1943.* *(NYK Line)*

195. **Taiyo Maru** *(14,457 tons, NYK Line). Ex-*Cap Finisterre *of Hamburg Sud-America,* Taiyo Maru *sailed on North Pacific routes.* *(NYK Line)*

141

196. **Haruna Maru** *(10,421 tons, NYK Line) was in service between Yokohama and Hamburg from 1922 to 1939. Lost in July 1942.* *(NYK Line Official)*

197. **Viet-Nam** *(13,162 tons, MM) dates from 1951 and was one of a series of ships for the French – Far East service.* *(Artist: Roger Chapelet. Publisher: Messageries Maritime)*

142

198. **Patris** *(18,860 tons, Chandris). Purchased as* Bloemfontein Castle *in 1959 she operated for* Chandris on the Greece to Sydney route. *(Artist: Derrick Smoothy. Publisher: Chandris)*

THE SS MONTEREY, 632 FEET LONG; 79 FEET BREADTH; GROSS TONNAGE 19,000; SPEED 22½ KNOTS

199. **Monterey** *(18,017 tons, Matson) became* Matsonia *(1956) and* Lusline *(1963) before her sale to* Chandris in 1970 (see No.200). *(Matson)*

143

200. **Britanis** *(18,254 tons, Chandris) is the* Monterey *in another guise. She became the oldest liner in service in 1985, being built in 1931.* *(Artist: Derrick Smoothy. Publisher: Chandris)*

CHAPTER 7

The Postcard Artists

Although the subject of British maritime painting has received more attention from art historians in the last two decades, the number of books solely devoted to it remains small. The usual origin identified for British maritime art is the work of two Dutchmen, father and son, who flourished in England during the reign of King Charles II. They were **Willem van de Velde** the Elder (1611-1693) and his son of the same name (1633-1707). Usually known as the Elder and the Younger, they painted in a studio situated in what is now the National Maritime Museum at Greenwich on the outskirts of London. The influence of these two Dutchmen spread through the eighteenth century and there were a number of outstanding British artists who emerged at that time. Among them were **Peter Monamy** (1670-1749) and **Nicholas Pocock** (1741-1821), the Bristol sea captain who turned to art as a profession.

The Victorians were insatiable in their demand for pictures and the nineteenth century saw some of the greatest names in British art displaying their talents on canvas and in watercolour. Among them were the giants **John Constable** and **J.M.W. Turner.** A very clear British school developed during that century, leading various styles.

Towards the end of the century, when the postcard was just becoming familiar to people in all walks of life, there emerged two British artists who, apart from being outstanding in their own field, also sold work to shipping companies. These were **Charles Dixon** and **William Wyllie.** Both men achieved fame in their own lifetime and today their paintings fetch many thousands of pounds on the rare occasions they come on to the market. In parallel with the professional artist, about the turn of the century the demand for artwork for postcards became so great that a new generation of artists grew up. These are loosely described as 'poster artists' and, because their skills in producing quick, attractive and accurate sketches of liners could best be sold in ports, many of them were based in places like Liverpool.

Among painters located in Liverpool in the early years of this century were **Walter Thomas, Sam Brown, James Mann** and **Odin Rosenvinge.** All these produced postcards for various shipping companies and much of their work can be found in Liverpool museums and art galleries as their legacy to us today.

There follows an alphabetical list of all identified artists of the illustrations that appear in this book, together with a short biography and the illustrations credited to the artist.

BLACK, Montague Birrell b. 1889

Little seems to be known of this very able artist who painted many postcards for the White Star Line, particularly just before the First World War and who has a very attractive style. He lived in Liverpool.

Nos. 74, 75 and 141

BROWN, Samuel John Milton 1873-1963

Sam Brown was born in Liverpool on 13 April 1873, the son of Edward Brown, a dispensing chemist and Post Master who was an outstanding amateur artist. Brown senior encouraged his son to become an artist and when he left Liverpool College at the age of fourteen he was apprenticed to a firm of

145

lithographic artists. Sam Brown spent all his spare time around Liverpool docks learning the 'feel' of ships and, because many sailing vessels still used the port in those years, it is said of him that he quite often spent hours aloft studying the rigging of these magnificent vessels.

He studied art at the Liverpool School of Art and then, throughout a long career as a Liverpool artist, he made his living by painting maritime subjects and supplying artwork to shipping companies. Some of his most attractive work was done for postcards and in particular the work that he produced for Thomas Forman and Sons in Nottingham, is much valued by the collector.

Much of his life Brown lived in Wallasey but on the death of his father in 1936 he moved to North Wales. Sadly, in his later years he suffered from increasing blindness and, like many artists, he was in somewhat reduced circumstances. He died in 1963 in his ninetieth year.

Nos. 18, 27, 29, 34, 35, 41, 44, 50, 80, 87, 139 and 140

CHAPELET, Roger

Roger Chapelet was a poster artist working in Paris in the late 1950s to early 1960s.

Nos. 20 and 197

CHURCH, Bernard W.

Bernard Church is best known for his aviation and shipping postcards which he designed for the publishers J. Salmon and Company. He was active around the period of the Second World War.

No. 117

DIXON, Charles, RI   1872-1934

Charles Dixon was born at Goring in Surrey and had his first work accepted by the Royal Academy at the age of sixteen. He was elected to the RI at the age of twenty-eight and made his living by working as a commercial artist for the *Graphic* and other magazines of the period. He addressed himself to all kinds of maritime subjects and was particularly happy in watercolours. Himself a keen yachtsman, he had a great knowledge of sailing ships and in 1901 he co-operated with C.N. Robinson to produce a book called *Britannia's Bulwarks* which was packed with Dixon's illustrations of historical sailing ships and contemporary warships. He supplied many paintings for various postcard companies and appears in this volume frequently.

Today Dixon's work is much sought after and fetches very large sums at auction, particularly his watercolours of shipping scenes on the Thames which are especially attractive.

Nos. 9, 14, 21-22, 24-26, 33, 71, 73, 76, 89-93, 95, 119-120, 138, 174, 180-182 and 189

FRY, John H.

John Fry was another artist who produced shipping scenes for the publishers J. Salmon and Company. His style is primitive and, to some tastes, unattractive.

No. 113

GRIBBLE, Bernard Finegan   1873-1962

Bernard Gribble was born in London, the son of an architect who designed Brompton Oratory. He followed his father into the architectural profession but later turned to painting and exhibited at the Royal Academy from 1891 to 1904. In his later years he lived in Dorset.

No. 183

HOPKINSON, C.F.

C.F. Hopkinson was an artist used by Cunard in the late 1940s and his work appears on postcards published by Forman and Sons for the Cunard Company.

No. 67

de LACEY, Charles   c.1885-1930

Charles de Lacey is best known as a press artist for the *Illustrated London News* and he also, for a time, had an appointment as an official artist to the Port of London Authority. He exhibited at the Royal Academy and is known for his studies of the River Thames and its scenery. His work is often compared to that of W.L. Wyllie (q.v.).

No. 188

LACHOTTE, Marchard L.

Marchard Lachotte was a French poster artist working in the 'Art Deco' period.

No. 116

MCDOWELL William John Patton   1888-1950

William McDowell was born in Barrow-in-Furness and grew up there. Like many another Barrow schoolboy, he left school at fourteen and served an apprenticeship at the famous Vickers Shipyard. He entered the drawing office at Vickers and this is, perhaps, why his paintings look so accurate and precise. Certainly he grew to know all about the construction of ships while at the Barrow yard.

Following the end of the First World War he left Vickers and became a full-time marine artist, specialising in commercial work for large shipping companies, although he accepted a number of private commissions. McDowell is another artist whose work is now recognised by collectors and much sought after.

Nos. 17, 83, 86, 88, 147-150

MANN, James Scrymgeour, RI, PRCA   1883-1946

James Mann was of Scots origin, born in Dundee, and was son and grandson of captains in the merchant service. The family maintained the sea-going tradition by James' brother, Robert, who became Commodore of the Bibby Line. Mann served in the First World War in which he was wounded and afterwards he always walked with a limp. Following his war service he studied at the Liverpool School of Art, coming to Liverpool because of his great interest in shipping.

Mann was a great watercolourist and the delicate nature of many of his marine paintings give them a special air of authority. He produced postcard artwork for all the main Liverpool companies including Cunard and White Star, and a particularly attractive series for Bibby Line. Much of his Cunard work was published by Forman and Sons.

In 1942 he was elected President of the Royal Cambrian Academy, an honour which gave him much pleasure. He died in Llandudno in 1946. Today his work is known far beyond Liverpool and is attractive to collectors.

Nos. 154, 186 and 187

MASON, Frank, RI   1876-1965

Frank Mason was born in Yorkshire and began his career at sea, being educated as a cadet on HMS *Conway*. He served in the Royal Navy in World War One and then became a war artist. A number of his pictures from this period are in the Imperial War Museum. He became a full-time artist between the two wars and worked as an illustrator, poster artist for railway companies and supplying posters and postcards for shipping companies. He exhibited at the Royal Academy from 1900 onwards and was elected RI in 1929.

Nos. 38-39, 170, 173 and 193

NICHOLSON, John   b.1920

John Nicholson is well known for his attractive colour illustrations in many of today's shipping magazines. He lives and works in Leeds and is particularly well known for his illustrations of paddle-steamers and ocean liners. His early work for J. Salmon and Company is now the target of collectors.

Nos. 19, 132 and 184

OLIVER, Richard
Little appears to be known of this artist and his work.

No. 142

PENNINGTON, Oswald F.

This artist's stylistic but attractive work appeared in the mid-1920s for the Canadian Pacific Steamship Company. The author has not found it used elsewhere and has been unsuccessful in discovering details of his career.

Nos. 126-129

ROSENVINGE, Odin   1880-1957

Born at Newcastle upon Tyne of Danish decent, Rosenvinge was brought up with the sea in his background. He had a natural ability for art and, when he left school, following a short time as a trainee reporter, he joined a Leeds commercial art and printing firm. When he was thirty-two he moved to Liverpool and joined the firm of Turner and Dunnett who had clients among all the major shipping companies. Here he worked together with Walter Thomas (q.v.) who acted as his assistant.

Odin Rosenvinge was one of the most prolific of the poster artists and developed a clear style of his own. His experience in the Middle East, where he served during the First World War, led him to use brighter colours to get good effects and much of his work which dates from the 1920s contains striking tones of orange. Later on in life, when he was in his fifties, his employers went into liquidation and Rosenvinge turned to freelance. At the height of his powers, his work ranks with anything that Dixon or Spurling could produce and it is surprising that he is so little known among conventional maritime art collectors.

Nos. 25, 28, 31, 37, 40, 43, 48, 55, 64, 100, 123-124, 133, 137, 159, 165, 191

SHOESMITH, Kenneth Denton, RI   1890-1939

Born in Halifax in Yorkshire, Kenneth Shoesmith was brought up in Blackpool and showed early talent as an artist. He decided to make a career at sea and became a cadet on HMS *Conway*. On leaving *Conway* he joined the Royal Mail Line and, while he followed the career of a Merchant Officer with that well-known company, he continued his enthusiasm for drawing and painting. He was mostly self taught but undertook a correspondence course early in his career as an artist and seems to have derived great benefit from this.

Shoesmith's style changed considerably during his life as a comparison of his work illustrated in this volume will show. In his early years he had a natural flowing style but this became more in the 'Art Deco' mode later on. Between the wars he worked for the publishers Thomas Forman who had sole rights to producing Cunard postcards and much attractive work survived. There is also a collection of this work in the Ulster Museum, Belfast.

Nos. 32, 45-46, 52-54 and 156-158

SILAS, Ellis   1883-1971

Ellis Silas, born in 1883, was a watercolour painter who specialised in marine subjects and spent considerable time in the Far East. He has pictures currently held in the collection of the National Maritime Museum and he exhibited at the Royal Academy and Royal Institute.

No. 162

SMITH, John S.   fl.1940s-1950s

John Smith is a contemporary artist who has exhibited at the RSMA.

No. 131

SMOOTHY, Derrick O.

Derrick Smoothy is a contemporary artist who has exhibited at the RSMA from 1950 and is well known for his portraits of modern ocean liners. Enquiries about his work can be made to the Parker Gallery, Pimlico Road, London, SW1.

Nos. 198 and 200

SPURLING, John Robert Charles (Jack)   1870-1933

Jack Spurling was born in Suffolk on 12 December 1870. His father was a jute merchant and it was this trade that gave the boy his first taste of the sea. His talent as an artist showed early and he himself said that his one pleasure as a boy was painting ships and he spent many of his holidays along the London dock side. He went to sea under sail at the age of sixteen and in the following years gained the knowledge and experience which led him to produce a series of paintings of square riggers which remain unmatched for their realism and popularity. As a painter of ships' portraits, Spurling has no equal and the series of postcards which he produced for P&O remains among the best ever published by a shipping company. Five examples are given in this book.

After seven years at sea, Spurling came ashore to practice, in turn, marine painting and then acting. At the latter profession he enjoyed some success and he never seemed to have been in any economic difficulty all his life. Later on, his attention turned more and more to painting and before he died at the age of sixty-two he had produced some of the best marine paintings ever. Much of his work was destroyed during the Second World War and is now very rare.

Nos. 175-179

THOMAS, Walter, ARCA   1894-1971

As we have seen earlier, Walter Thomas worked with Odin Rosenvinge in Liverpool for much of his career, of which we know very little. He did much work for the Blue Funnel Line and worked for them for most of his career. After acting as an Admiralty artist during the Second World War he went freelance in the 1950s when he moved from Liverpool to live in the Isle of Man.

Nos. 42, 47, 79, 81, 84-85, 101, 137, 164 and 190

TURNER, Charles E.   1993-1965

Charles Turner was another Liverpool artist, Lancastrian born, whose work in the 1920s for Taylor, Garnett, Evans and Company led to a series of excellent postcards. Later his work was used by Thomas Forman and his pictures of *Queen Mary* and *Queen Elizabeth* for Cunard are full of action. He served in the Royal Air Force in World War One and as a war artist in World War Two. His battle pictures of the loss of *Bismarck* and *Scharnhorst* are in the National Maritime Museum, Greenwich. He died in Looe, Cornwall on 14 April 1965.

Nos. 49, 56-63, 65-66, 68-70 and 143

WILKINSON, Norman, CBE, PRI   1878-1971

Norman Wilkinson was born in Cambridge but the family moved to Portsmouth and he studied at the Portsmouth School of Art and also at St. Ives. He did early work for the *Illustrated London News* and worked for them until he entered the Royal Navy during the First World War. After the war he emerged as one of the best known poster designers in the country, working for shipping and railway companies. He was a keen yachtsman but also very interested in aviation and during the Second World War served in the Royal Air Force. His work covers every aspect of maritime life and continues to grow in popularity.

Nos. 1 and 163

WYLLIE, William Lionel, RA   1851-1931

Born in London to an artistic family, Wyllie was educated at the Royal Academy School which he joined in 1865. He exhibited his first painting at the Academy in 1868. Wyllie had an excessive love of the sea and his output is prolific, covering all kinds of maritime subjects but with a great interest in the Royal Navy and historic occasions. He does not seem to have engaged in much work of a poster or postcard nature but a series he supplied to P&O in the first decade of this century is quite charming and two examples are illustrated in this book. Among his many interests Wyllie, who lived at Portsmouth in his later years, was a member of the committee that carried out the restoration of HMS *Victory* under preservation in a dry-dock in Portsmouth dockyard.

Nos. 169, 171

Bibliography

Postcards

There is a considerable library of published books on postcards available. The following list is by no means exhaustive but lists books which the author has found useful.

Byatt, Anthony: *Picture Postcards and their Publishers*, Malvern 1978

Carline, Richard, *Collecting Picture Postcards*, Malvern 1982

Coysh, A.W.: *The Dictionary of Picture Postcards*, Woodbridge 1984

Davies, Pete: *Collecting Modern Postcards*, Nottingham 1987

Staff, Frank: *The Picture Postcard and its Origins*, London 1966

Staff, Frank: *Picture Postcards and Travel*, Guildford 1979

Also essential to the serious collector is the use of a good up-to-date postcard catalogue:

Mead, Venman and Brooks: *RF Picture Postcard Catalogue*, published periodically

Ocean Liners

The published bibliography on ocean passenger vessels is vast, but two standard works in collected volume form are currently available for the researcher which should meet most needs:

Bonsor, N.R.P.: *North Atlantic Seaway*, Brookside-Patrick Stephens, 1976, Vols. 1-5 inclusive

Bonsor, N.R.P.: *South Atlantic Seaway*, Brookside-Patrick Stephens, 1983

Kludas, Arnold, *Great Passenger Ships of the World*, Patrick Stephens 1976-86, Vols. 1-6

Abbreviations

ARCA – Associate of the Royal Cambrian Academy

B&I – British India Steam Navigation Company

CBE – Commander of the British Empire

CGT – The French Line

GPO – General Post Office

HAL – Holland-America Line

MM – Messageries Maritime

NDL – Norddeutsche Lloyd (North German Lloyd)

NYK – Nippon Yusen Kabusiki Kaisya

NZ – New Zealand

P&O – Peninsular and Oriental Steam Navigation Company

PRI – President, Royal Institute of Painters in Watercolours

PSN – Pacific Steam Navigation

RA – Royal Academy

RI – Royal Institute

RSMA – Royal Society of Marine Artists

PRCA – President, Royal Cambrian Academy

Index

Page numbers in bold refer to illustrations and captions

Aconcagua, 128
Adda, 110, **120**
Adelaide, 124
Adolf Woermann, 112, **112**
Adriatic, 12, 33, **64**
Adriatic, 24
Aegean Sea, **100**
Africa, 12, 136
  East, 105, 136, **140**
  North, 129
  South, 23, 105-112
  West, 110, **111, 120**
Alaunia, **50,** 99, 100
Albania, 21, **46,** 99
Albany, 94
Alberta, 94
Alcantara, 113-114, **118**
Aldershot, 15
Alexandria, 122, 128
Allan Line, 16, 19, 88, 90,
  89-91, 93, 97
Allan, Sir Hugh, 88
Alsatian, 88, **91**
Amazon, River, 115, **119**
America, 12, 129
  North, 11, 17-87
  South, 28, 105, **114,** 115,
  131
America, 136
American Line, 11, 16, 30,
  72, 83, 94
Anchor Donaldson, **77**
Anchor Line, 27-28, **75-76,**
  134, **139**
Andania, 22, **34, 49,** 99-100
Anderson, Arthur, 105, 122
Andes, 113, 115, **116, 121**
Anselm, 115, **119**
Antonia, 100
Antwerp, 27, **71**
Aquitania, 20, **43-44, 55**

Arabia, 17, 124
Arabic, 27, **71**
Arcadia, 129
Arcadian, 113, **116**
Argentina, 28, 114, 115
Art Deco, **34, 39,** 147, 149
Arundel Castle, 109, **109**
Ascania, **50,** 99-101, **104**
Asia, 12
Asturias, 113. 114, **116**
Athenia, 28, **77**
Atlantic Ocean
  North, 11, 17-104
  South, 105-121, 132
Atlantic Transport Line, 16,
  26-27, **74,** 94
Atlantis, 113, **116**
Aurania, **49, 57,** 99, 100
Aureol, 110
Ausonia, 99, 100
Australasia, 12, 122-144
Australia, 23, **77,** 101, 122,
  123, 124, 125, 131, 136
Australia, 122, 124, **125**
Avila (Star), 115, **119**
Avon, River, 17
Avonmouth, 90, 94, **98**
Azores, **36, 119**

Balkans, 18
Ballard, Dr. Robert, 25
Ballin, Albert, 29-30, **82**
Balranald, **125,** 128
Baltic, 24, **63**
Barcelona, **69**
Barrow-in-Furness, 88, 147
Barton, **98-100**
Bates, Sir Percy, 100
Beaver Line, 88
Beira, 136
Belfast, 24, **87,** 94, 107, 129,

149
Belgenland, 27, **73**
Belgium, 27
Berengaria, 21, **44, 45, 55,** 91
Bergen, 12
Berlin, 29, **71, 81**
Bibby Line, 134, **137,** 147
Binns, Jack, 24
Birch, J., 15
Biscay, Bay of, 125
Bishop Rock, **42**
Bismarck, 26, 150
Black, Montague Birrell, 11,
  63-64, 103, 145
Black Sea, 128
Blackpool, 148
Bloemfontein Castle, **143**
Blue Anchor Line, 128, **136**
Blue Funnel Line, 134, **139,**
  149
Blue Riband, **19,** 20, 23, 29,
  32, 33, **62, 78, 79, 84, 86,**
  97
Blue Star Line, 112, 115, **119**
Bombay, 122, 124, 125, **127,**
  134
Booth Line, 112, 115, **119**
Boston, 18, **42, 46,** 94, 100
Brazil, 28
Bremen, 28
Bremen, 29, **80**
Bremerhaven, 13
Bristol, 17, **24,** 90, 94, **98,**
  145
Britanis, 136, **144**
Britannia, 17
Britannic, **19,** 26, **70**
British Admiralty, 20, 124,
  149
British and American Steam
  Navigation Co., **18**

British and Commonwealth
Shipping Co., 109
British Government, 17, 20,
22, 105
British India Steam
Navigation Co., 125-126
British International Postcard
Exhibition, 14
Briton, 105
Brown & Co., John, 20, 22,
101
Brown, Samuel John Milton,
11, 12, **34, 38-39, 42, 45,
47, 50, 66, 70, 102-103,**
145-146
Brunel, Isambard Kingdom,
17, **18**
Buenos Aires, 112, 114, **118**
Burma, 134
Byatt, Anthony, 16

Cadiz, 122
Caird, 125
Cairo, 90
Calais, 125
Calcutta, 107
Caledonia, 27, **75, 76,** 124
Calgarian, **91**
Cambridge, 150
Campania, 18, **30, 36, 37**
Canada, 88-104
Canadian National Line, **100**
Canadian Northern Line, 97,
98-99
Canadian Northern Railway,
90
Canadian Pacific Railway, 88
Canadian Pacific Steamships
Limited, 16, 88, **89,** 90, **90-
97,** 96-97, 101, 148
Canberra, 129
Cap Finisterre, **141**
Cape Government, 107
Cape Horn, 107, **113,** 132
Cape Matapan, **41**
Cape of Good Hope, 105,
110, 128
Cape Town, 105, 107, 109,
128, 136
Capetown Castle, 109, **111**

Captain Cook, **77**
Caribbean, 13, **24,** 28
Carinthia, **58,** 101, **104**
Carmania, 19, 23, **31, 38-39,
54, 61,** 101
Carnarvon Castle, 109
Caronia, 19, 23, **37, 61,** 101
Carpathia, **42**
Castalia, 134, **139**
Castle Line, 105, 107
Cedric, 24, **31, 63**
'Celebrated Liners Series',
11, 15, **31**
Celt, 105, **107,** 108
Celtic, 24
CGT – *see* French Line
Chandris Line, 136, **143-144**
Chapelet, Roger, **35, 142,** 146
Charles II, King, 145
Cherbourg, 91
Chicago, 11
Chile, 132
China, 97, **117, 123,** 124
China, 124, **124**
China Sea, 124
Church, Bernard W., **85,** 146
Churchill, Winston, 22
Chusan, 129
City of Chester, **20**
City of Nagpur, **140**
City of New York, 18
City of Paris, 18, 30, **83,** 136,
140
Clan Line, 109
Clyde, River, 20, 22, 28, 101
Cobh, **37**
Columbus, 26, 29, **33, 67, 80,**
94
Comorin, 129, **130**
Constable, John, 145
Conte di Savoia, 33
Conway, HMS, 148
Cook, Captain James, 122
Coronel, Battle of, **133**
Cornwall, **83,** 150
Craddock, Admiral, 132
Crete, 126
Crippen, Dr., 88
Cunard Line, 11-13, 15-23,
26-28, **30-31,** 33, **34-61,**

91-92, 97, 100-101, **104,**
107, 122, 147, 149, 150
Cunard, Sam, 17
Cunard White Star, 26
Cunning, Neville, **115**
Currie, Sir Donald, 105, 107-
109, **108**
Cyril, **119**

Dalmatian coast, 12
Damant, Commander G.C.,
96
Dane, 105
Danube, 113, **115**
Delhi, 124
Delta, 124
Detroit, 11
Deutsche Ost Afrika – *see*
German East Africa Line
Deutschland, 30, **82**
Devanha, **123,** 124
Dido, 134
Dixon, Charles, 11, 12, **26,
31, 35-38, 41, 62-64, 71-
74, 86-87, 102, 127, 133-
134, 138,** 145, 146, 148
Dixon, J. Arthur, 13, 15
Dominion Line, **73-74,** 92,
94, 97
Dominion, 94
Donaldson Line, 16, 28, **76,**
88
Dongola, 124
Donitz, Admiral, **48**
Doric, 26, **69**
Dorset, 146
Dorset, 126, **138**
Dover, 125
Dover Castle, 107
Drake, Sir Francis, 122
Dresden, 29, **80**
Drottningholm, **89**
Dunbar Castle, 109, **110**
Duncan & Co., Robert, 17
Dundee, 16, 147
Durban, 107, 128

Edinburgh, 10
Edinburgh Castle, **32**
Edward VII, King, 10

Egypt, 128
Egypt, 124, 125, **127**
Egyptian Rail Steamship Co., 90
Elder Dempster Line, **24**, 110, **120**
Ellerman Line, 134, 136, **140**
Ellerman, Sir John, 136
Empress of Britain, 88, 90, 96
Empress of Canada, 90, **95**, 101
Empress of England, 90, **96**
Empress of France, **91**
Empress of Ireland, 88, **92**, 96
Empress of Japan, **97**
Empress of Scotland, 90, **95**, **97**
English Channel, **66, 110**, **127**
Essendon, Lord, 114
Etruria, 18, **36**
Eugénie, Empress, 107
Europa, 29, **80, 81**
Evans, Sir Francis, 108

Fairfield, **21**
Fairland, 101
Fairwind, 101
Falmouth, 91
Far East, **35, 78**, 122-144, 149
Federal Steam Navigation Co., 126, **138**
Fedor Chaliapin, 101
Fernando Port, **111**
Florida, 13
Florida, 24, **64**
Forman, Thomas, 15, **34, 38, 44-45, 47, 48, 50-52, 59-61, 104, 140**, 146, 147, 149, 150
France, **142**
France, 13
Franconia, 20-21, **42, 51-52**, 101
French Line, 13, 32-33, **81, 85**
Fry, John H., **83**, 146
Furness, Sir Christopher. 91

Gale & Polden, 15
Gallipoli, 26, **100**, 124
Garth Castle, 108
Geestemunde, **79**
General Post Office, 10, 11
Georgic, 26, **70**
German, 107
German East Africa Line, **25**, 110
Germanic, **19**
Germany, 91, 100, 132
Empress of, **95**
Gibraltar, 122, 134, **139**
Glasgow, 15, **21**, 27, **75**, 88, 97, 134
Gneisenau, 129
Gold Coast, 110
Goring, 146
Gotheborg Litho AB, **89**
Govan, **86**
'Grand Tour', 11
Grantully Castle, 108, **108**
Graphic, 146
Great Britain, 17
Great Western, 17, **18**
Great Western Railway Co., 17
Great Western Steam Ship Co., 17
Greece, **143**
Green Goddess, 23, 61
Greenock, **20, 23**, 125, 128
Greenwich, 145
Greiff, 113
Gribble, Bernard Finegan, **135**, 146
Gripsholm, **81**
Guang Ha, **117**

H&J Ltd, **118**
Halifax (Nova Scotia), 17, **76**, 91, 96, 97
Halifax (Yorkshire), 148
Hamburg, 30, **82**
Hamburg, **84**, 107, 110, **112**, **142**
Hamburg-Amerika Line, 16, 24, 28-30, **82**
Hamburg Sud-America, **141**
'Hands Across the Sea'

series, 11
Handyside and Henderson, 27
Hapag, **82, 93**
Harland & Wolff, 24, **86**, 114, **137**
Hartmann, F., 15
Hartung, **112**
Haruna Maru, 136, **142**
Hawaii, 136
Haworth, James, **101**
Hebrides, 132
Heliopolis, 90
Highland Brigade, 114
Highland Chieftain, 114
Highland Hope, 114
Highland Monarch, 114
Highland Patriot, 114
Highland Princess, 114, **117**
Highland Rover, **118**
Himalaya, 122-124, **123, 129**
Hoffmann, C.R., 15
Holland, 33
Holland-America Line, 33, **72, 86-87, 93**
Holt & Co., Alfred, 134
Homeric, 26, **33, 67**
Hong Kong, 122, 124
Hopkinson, C.F. **60**, 147
Horne Lines, **89**
Hudson River, **68**

Iceland, 100
Ile de France, 33, **85**
Illustrated London News, 147, 150
Imperator, 21, **44**, 91
Imperial War Museum, 148
Inchcape, Lord, 125, 126
India, 122-125, **123**, 129, 134, 136, 140
India, 124, 126
Inman Line, 18, **20**, 30, **83**
Inman, William, 20
International Mercantile Marine Co., 94
International Postcard Dourfe, 14
Ireland, 28, 130
Isandalwana, 107
Islay, 132

Isle of Man, 149
Isle of Wight, 13, 15, **80**
Ismay, Bruce, 24
Ismay, Thomas, 23-24
Italia Line, 13, 33, **86**
Italy, 101, **138**
Ivernia, 30, **41,** 101

Japan, **97,** 136, **141**

Kaisar-I-Hind, 125, **128**
Kaiser Wilhelm der Grosse,
  28, **78, 79**
Kaiser Wilhelm II, 29, **79**
Kaiserin Auguste Victoria, **95**
Karlsruhe, **22**
Kashmir, 132
Kendall, Captain, 88
Kennedy, Captain, 129
  Ludovic, 129
Khedive Ismail, 128, **140**
Khedivial Mail Line, 128
Kinfauns Castle, **106,** 108
Kinsale, Old Head of, 21
Kloster, 13
Konig Albert, 28, **78**
Kronprinz Wilhelm, 29, **79**
Kronprinzessin Cecilie, 19
Kylsant, Lord, 113-114

Lacey, Charles de, **138,** 147
Lachotte, Marchard L., **85,**
  147
Laconia, 21, **47, 48, 57**
Lamport & Holt, 115, **120**
Lancashire, 92, 150
Lancastria, 22, **51**
Lankhout, **86-87**
Laos, **35**
Lapland, 27, **71**
Laurentic, 26, **69,** 96, 97, **102**
Le Havre, 13
Leeds, 148
Leonid Sobinov, 61, 101
Letitia, 28, **76, 77**
Leviathan, 30, 32, **83**
Leyland and Atlantic
  Transport Line, 24, 94
Liberia, 13
Liberté, 29, **81**

Liguria, **93**
Lisbon, 122
Liverpool, 11-12, 15-17, **20,**
  22-23, **42, 46,** 88, 91-92,
  94, 96-97, 100-101, 107,
  110, 112, 114-115, 134,
  136, **137,** 145-150
  Bar Lightship, **50**
  College, 145
  School of Art, 146, 147
Liverpool and Mississippi
  Steamship Co., 92
Liverpool P&S, **120**
Llandudno, 147
Lloyds, 125
London, 14, 15, **74,** 99, 107,
  112, 114, **118,** 124, **127,**
  131, 132, 149
Londonderry, 94
Looe, 150
Lourenzo Marques, **25**
Lucania, 18, **30**
Lund's Blue Anchor Line –
  see Blue Anchor Line
Lusitania, 20, 21, **39**
Lusline, **143**

MacBrayne, David, 12
McDowell, William John
  Patton, **33, 68-70, 108-111,**
  147
Majestic, 18, 23, 26, **62, 67,**
  68
Majorca, **67**
Malin Head, 96
Malohja, 128
Malta, **126**
Manacles, **83**
Manaos, 115, **119**
Manchester, 91
Manchester Liners Limited,
  91, **101**
Manchester Regiment, 92,
  101
Manchester Ship Canal, 91,
  101
Manhattan, 32, **84**
Mann, James Scrymgeour,
  11, **114, 137,** 145, 147
Mann, Robert, 147

Mantua, 125, **127**
Marco Polo, 122
Marconi, 24
Mardi Gras, **96**
Marglen, 90, **93**
Marloch, **89**
Marseilles, 124, 125
Mason, Frank, **44, 125, 127,**
  140, 148
Massachusetts, 94
Matson Line, 136, **143**
Matsonia, **143**
Mauretania, 20, 22, **40, 54,**
  60
Mediterranean, 12, 18, **42,**
  91, 128, **139, 140**
Megantic, 96-97, **103**
Meier, H., 28
Melita, 90, **93**
Messageries Maritime, 13,
  35, 142
Mexico, Gulf of, 92
Miami, 13, **96**
Michelangelo, 13
Middle East, 148
Millar & Long, 15
Minneapolis, 27, **74**
Minnesota, 27, **74**
Mississippi, 92
Monamy, Peter, 145
Mongolia, **23,** 128, **129**
Monterey, 136, **143-144**
Montevideo, 112
Montlaurier, 90, **94**
Montreal, 88, 90, 92, 94, 97
Mooltan, 125, **126,** 129, **132**
Morgan, John Pierpoint, 19,
  24, 26-27, 94
Murmeister & Johler, **111**
Mussolini, 33

Napier engines, 17
Narrung, 128, **136**
Natal, 105, 107
National Maritime Museum,
  Greenwich, 145, 149, 150
Needles, **80**
Nelson Line, 112, 114, **117-**
  118
New York, 14, 15, 17, 18, 23,

25, 27, **42, 43, 47, 71, 74-75, 78, 84,** 88, 91, 96-97, 115, 134
World Fair, **60**
New York, 82
New Zealand, 126, **138**
New Zealand Line, **129**
New Zealand Shipping Co., 126, **138**
Newcastle upon Tyne, 11, 15, 148
Newfoundland, 100, **104**
Nicholson, John, 13, **34, 97,** **135,** 148
Nigeria, 110
Nippon Yusen Kabusiki Kaisya (NYK) Line, 136, **141-142**
Norddeutscher Lloyd – *see* North German Lloyd
Normandie, 33, **67, 85**
North Cape, 12
North German Lloyd, 16, 18, **21, 22,** 24, 28-29, **78-81, 94**
North Sea, 129, 132
Northland, **74**
Nortucket, **64**
Norway, 12, **80**
Norway, 13
Norwegian Caribbean Lines, 13
Nottingham, 15, 146
Nova Scotia, **76,** 91, 97

Oceanic, 23, **26, 62**
Oceanic Steam Navigation Co. Ltd, 23
OILETTE Series – *see* Tuck
Oliver, Richard, **104,** 148
Olympic, 24, 25, **27, 29, 65-66**
Orbita, **113,** 115
Orcades, 134, **135**
Oriana, 134
Orient, 131
Orient Line (Orient Steam Navigation Co.), 128, 129, 131-134, **133-135**

Orient Pacific, 16
Ormonde, 134, **135**
Orontes, 131-132, **133**
Orvieto, 132, **134**
Oslo, 13
Otranto, 132, **133, 134**
Otway, 132
Oxfordshire, 134, **137**

P&O Branch Line, 128, **136**
Pacific Ocean, 88, 126, 136, **138, 141**
Pacific Steam Navigation, 112, **113-114,** 114-115, 131
Panama, 13, **129**
Paris, 146
Parker Gallery, 149
Parsons, Charles, 19
Patris, 136, **143**
Peninsular and Oriental Steam Navigation Co. (P&O), 11-13, **23,** 101, 105, 122-134, **123-132,** 132, 134, **136,** 149, 150
Peninsular Steam Navigation Co., 122
Pennington, Oswald F., **93-95,** 148
Pennland, 27, **72, 73**
Persia, 17, 124, 126
Pharaonic Co., 128, **140**
Philadelphia, 26
Philadelphia, 30, **83**
Philipps, Owen, 113
Piraeus, 136
Pittsburgh, 11
Pittsburgh, **72,** 97
Plate, River, 114, 115
Pocock, Nicholas, 145
Port Glasgow, 17
Port of London Authority, 147
Port Said, **73, 112,** 122, 125
Portsmouth, 17, 150
School of Art, 150
Portugal, 114
Pretoria, 112
Pridday, C.M., **62**
Prinz Phratric Wilhelm, **94**
Prohibition, 30-32

QE2, 13, 23, 33
Quebec, **77,** 88, 90, 92, 97, 100, **103-104**
Queen Elizabeth, 13, 22-23, 33, **59,** 150
Queen Mary, 13, 21-23, **44, 59,** 150
Queenstown, **37,** 94

Rafaello, 13
Rajputana, 129, **130**
Rangoon, **137**
Rawalpindi, 129, **130**
Red Sea, 122
Red Star Line, 26-27, **71-73, 74,** 94, 97, **103**
Regina, **73,** 97, **103**
Reid, Andrew, 11, 15, **23, 24,** **113-114, 123**
Reina del Pacifico, **114,** 115
Rendell, Maurice, **32**
Republic, 24, **64,** 94
Rex, 33, **86**
Rio de Janeiro, 105, 112
Robinson, C.N., 146
Rodgers, Woodes, 122
Rosenvinge, Odin, 11, 12, **37, 39, 40, 43, 45-46, 48-49, 52, 58, 77, 90-91, 98, 117, 120, 139-140,** 145, 148, 149
Rotterdam, 33, **87**
Royal Academy, 146-150
Royal Air Force, 150
Royal Cambrian Academy, 147
Royal Caribbean Line, 13
Royal Edward, 90-91, **98, 100**
Royal George, 90-91, **98-99**
Royal Institute, 146, 148, 149
Royal Mail Steam Packet Co. (Royal Mail Steam Lines Ltd), 16, 105, 112-115, **115-118, 121,** 131, 148
Royal Naval Review, **115**
Royal Navy, 22, **50,** 96, 100, 148, 150
Royal Princess, 13
Royal Society of Marine Artists, 149

Ruahine, 126, **138**
Russia, **61**

St. Angelo, **126**
St. Ives, 150
St. Lawrence River, 77, 88,
91-92, **92**, 96-97, 100, **104**
St. Nazaire, **51**
Salmon & Co., J., 15, **34**, 83-
85, 97, 135, 146, 148
Samaria, 21, **46-48, 56**, 100-
101
Sander & Sohn, W., **79**
Saxon, 105, **106**, 108
Saxonia, **41, 61**, 101
Scharnhorst, 129, 150
Scot, 108
Scotia, 17
Scotian, **93**
Scotland, 12, 28, 107
Scotsman, 94
Scotts of Greenock, 128
Scythia, 21, **47-48, 56**, 100-
101
Sevenoaks, 15
Severn, River, 109
Seymour, **65**
Shaw Savill Line, **34**
Shetlands, **62**
Shoesmith, Kenneth Denton,
11, **41, 47-48, 51-52, 116-
117**, 148-149
Silas, Ellis, **119**, 149
Simpson, J., **127**
Singapore, 122
Sirius, 17, **18**
Sitmar Line, 101
Smith, Captain E.J., 24, **64**
Smith, John S., **96**, 149
Smoothy, Derrick O., 13,
143-144, 149
Sorima, 125
Southampton, 11, 12, 15, 23,
25, **84**, 90, 97, 99-101,
105, 110, 112, 136
Southern Cross, **34**
Sovereign of the Seas, 13
Soviet Union, 101
Spain, 122
Spee, Admiral Graf von, 132

Spithead, 19, 113, **115**
Spurling, John Robert
Charles (Jack), 12, **129-
132**, 148, 149
Staffordshire, 134, **137**
Statendam, 33, **87**
Steamship Amalgamation
Plan, 94
Stewart & Co., George, 10
Stirling, Sir Lionel, 129
Storstad, 88
Strathaird,
Straths, the, 129
Stuart, F.G.O., 11, 15
Stuttgart, **21**
Suez Canal, 110, 122, **124**,
134
Suffolk, 149
Sulzer diesels, **137**
Surrey, 146
Suwa Maru, 136, **141**
Swan Hunter, 20, 99
Sweden, 29, 33, **89**
Swedish America Line, **89**
Sydney, 97, 122, 132, **133**,
136, **143**
Sylvania, 101

Taiyo Maru, 136, **141**
Tanzania, 110
Taylor, Garnett, Evans & Co.,
15, 22, **37-38, 49-50, 53-
57**, 150
Teutonic, 18, **62**
Thames, River, 17, 146, 147
Thomas, Walter, 11, **46, 48,
66-69, 77, 101, 120**, 134,
139, 145, 148, 149
Thompsons, 131
Thor, 114, **120**
Titanic, 15, 20, 24-26, **28-29,
42, 64, 65**, 129
Tobruk, **93**
Trans-Atlantic Publishing
Co., **19**
Transylvania, 27, **75-76**
Tuck, Raphael, 11, 15
Tuck's OILETTE Series, 15,
**31, 39-40, 43, 62, 65, 78-
79, 83, 85, 89, 92, 102-**

103, 115, 127, 135
Turner & Dunnett, 16, **36, 39-
43, 46, 48-49, 52, 58, 77,
90-91, 104, 120, 139-140**,
148
Turner, Charles E., 12, 13,
15, 22, **49-50, 53-57, 59-
61, 104**, 150
Turner, J.M.W., 145
Tyne, River, 20
Tyrrhenia, **51**

U-boats, 21, 28, **41-42, 48**,
58, 91, 96, 100, **119**, 126,
130, 132, **139, 141**
Ubena, 112
Ulster Museum, Belfast, 149
Umbria, 18, **35**
Union Castle Line, 11, 16,
32, 105-110, **106-111**, 136
Union Line, 105, **106**, 108,
112
Union Steamship Co. of New
Zealand, 126-128
United States, 13, 32, **84**
United States of America, 12,
18, 30, 32
United States Lines, 30, **83-
84**, 136
United States Shipping Board
Estate Agency, 30
Ushant, **127**

Valentine & Sons, James, 16
Valparaiso, **113**
van de Velde, Willem, 145
Vandyck, 115, **120**
Vaterland, 30, **83**
Vestey family, 115
Viceroy of India, 129, **131**
Vickers, 88, 147
Victorian, 88, **89**
Victory, HMS, 150
Viet-Nam, **142**
Virginian, 19, 88, **89-90**
Volendam, 33, **86**
Voltaire, 115, **120**

Wadai, **111**, 112
Wales, 105, 146

Wallasey, 146
Wallsend-on-Tyne, 99
Walmer Castle, 107, **107**, 108
Waratah, 128, **136**
Wars
  Crimean, 105
  First World, 10, 12, 20-21,
    26-30, **74, 79,** 88-89, 91,
    96, 99-100, **100, 106,** 112-
    113, 124-126, **134,** 147,
    148, 150
  Franco-Prussian, 10
  Second World, 12-13, 16,
    22, 28, 33, **49, 75-77, 86-
    87,** 90, **97,** 100, 109, **110,**
    112, 114-115, **119-120,**

129, **130,** 132, 134, **135,**
  136, **142,** 149, 150
Zulu, 107
Washington, 32, **84**
Watussi, 112
West Indies, 112
Westernland, 27, **73**
White Star Line, 11, 15-16,
  18-19, 18-19, 22-27, **26-
  27, 31, 33, 62-70, 72,** 88,
  92, 94, 96-97, **102-103,**
  145, 147
White Star-Dominion Line,
  96-97
Wilcox, Brodie, 122
Wilkinson, Norman, **18, 119,** 150

Wilhelm II, Emperor, 20, 29
Wilson, President, 21
Windhuk, **25,** 112
Windsor Castle, 109
Wisconsin, **65**
Woermann, Adolf, 110, **111-
  112,** 112
Wyllie, William Lionel, **124,
  126,** 145, 147, 150

Yokohama, 88, **142**
Yorkshire, 148

Zeeland, **74**